Language Handbook Worksheets
Answer Key

Second Course

HOLT, RINEHART AND WINSTON
A Harcourt Education Company
Orlando • Austin • New York • San Diego • Toronto • London

Copyright © by Holt, Rinehart and Winston

All rights reserved. No part of this publication may be reproduced or transmitted in any form or by any means, electronic or mechanical, including photocopy, recording, or any information storage and retrieval system, without permission in writing from the publisher.

Requests for permission to make copies of any part of the work should be mailed to the following address: Permissions Department, Holt, Rinehart and Winston, 10801 N. MoPac Expressway, Building 3, Austin, Texas 78759.

HOLT, HRW, and the **"Owl Design"** are trademarks licensed to Holt, Rinehart and Winston, registered in the United States of America and/or other jurisdictions.

Printed in the United States of America

> If you have received these materials as examination copies free of charge, Holt, Rinehart and Winston retains title to the materials and they may not be resold. Resale of examination copies is strictly prohibited.

> Possession of this publication in print format does not entitle users to convert this publication, or any portion of it, into electronic format.

6 7 8 0607 17
4500690228

Table of Contents

Language Handbook 1:	The Parts of Speech	1
Language Handbook 2:	Agreement	4
Language Handbook 3:	Using Verbs	9
Language Handbook 4:	Using Pronouns	13
Language Handbook 5:	Using Modifiers	16
Language Handbook 6:	Phrases	18
Language Handbook 7:	Clauses	21
Language Handbook 8:	Sentences	23
Language Handbook 9:	Complements	26
Language Handbook 10:	Kinds of Sentences	28
Language Handbook 11:	Writing Effective Sentences	31
Language Handbook 12:	Capital Letters	35
Language Handbook 13:	Punctuation	40
Language Handbook 14:	Punctuation	45
Language Handbook 15:	Punctuation	48
Language Handbook 16:	Spelling	51
Language Handbook 17:	Glossary of Usage	54

LANGUAGE HANDBOOK 1: THE PARTS OF SPEECH

WORKSHEET 1
Identifying Nouns
EXERCISE A
1. people; hours; sleep
2. Edison
3. man; schedule; life
4. night; living
5. day
6. notebooks; notes; books; experiments
7. hours; sleep
8. powers; concentration
9. project; days; rest
10. definition; genius; inspiration; perspiration

EXERCISE B
1. Chinua Achebe; writer; Nigeria
2. Nobel Peace Prize; Mother Teresa; year
3. Tuesday; Margaret; job; Japan
4. team; (gold) medal; hockey; Olympics
5. girl; student; Colombia
6. baseball; Ellen; mitt; shoes
7. earrings; Debbie; birthday
8. Armand; chef; brother-in-law
9. Four; groups; Nigeria; Ibo; Hausa; Fulani; Yoruba
10. family; Empire State Building; New York City

WORKSHEET 2
Identifying and Using Pronouns
EXERCISE A
1. My; her; which; she; herself
2. this
3. Which; itself; one
4. that; everyone
5. Who; it; her

EXERCISE B *(Pronouns may vary.)*
1. Some
2. it
3. who
4. his
5. He
6. he
7. his
8. He
9. his
10. They
11. no one
12. his
13. Some
14. them
15. his
16. What
17. They
18. he or she
19. They
20. us
21. himself
22. they
23. his
24. it
25. himself

WORKSHEET 3
Identifying Adjectives
EXERCISE A *(If you classify possessive pronouns as adjectives, then answers that are underscored may be considered correct.)*
1. young; whimsical
2. <u>his</u>; humorous; many; foreign; unknown; <u>his</u>; native
3. <u>his</u>; first; popular; successful
4. <u>His</u>; quaint; rural; delightful
5. Most
6. These; supernatural
7. many; pleasant
8. Moorish
9. this; comfortable
10. long; literary

EXERCISE B *(The first item in a pair is the adjective. The second is the word modified. If you classify possessive pronouns as adjectives, then answers that are underscored may be considered correct.)*
1. unique—form; Japanese—poetry
2. short—poem; strong—emotion; vivid—image; few—words
3. English—translations; several—poems; Japanese—poems; <u>our</u>—<u>teacher</u>; <u>our</u>—<u>poet</u>; favorite—poet; brief—report
4. <u>Our</u>—<u>reports</u>; accurate—reports; two—hours
5. great—place
6. eager—I; <u>my</u>—<u>subject</u>; famous—poet
7. <u>his</u>—<u>poetry</u>; wonderful—poetry
8. excellent—tips; which—books; poetry—books
9. <u>My</u>—<u>teacher</u>; <u>her</u>—<u>poet</u>; favorite—poet; Japanese—poet
10. <u>My</u>—<u>friend</u>; best—friend; these—poets

Answer Key **1**

LANGUAGE HANDBOOK 1: THE PARTS OF SPEECH

WORKSHEET 4
Identifying and Using Action and Helping Verbs

EXERCISE A
1. arrives
2. played
3. towers
4. ran
5. dodged
6. did block
7. will defend
8. has scored
9. practice
10. have suggested

EXERCISE B *(Verbs will vary.)*
1. celebrated
2. lasts
3. left
4. should reach
5. enveloped
6. like
7. asked
8. may apply
9. will finish
10. will use

WORKSHEET 5
Identifying Linking and Helping Verbs

EXERCISE A
1. is
2. has become
3. are
4. has been
5. remains
6. is considered
7. is
8. became
9. was
10. *Is*, is

EXERCISE B
1. <u>is</u>
2. <u>is</u>; <u>is</u>
3. <u>will</u> look
4. <u>becomes</u>
5. <u>are</u> made
6. <u>will</u> appear
7. <u>smells</u>; <u>is</u>
8. <u>is</u>
9. <u>should be</u>; <u>can be</u>
10. <u>has</u> become

WORKSHEET 6
Identifying and Using Adverbs

EXERCISE A *(The first item in a pair is the adverb. The second is the word or words modified.)*
1. seldom—varies
2. never—freezes
3. unusually—large
4. very—clear
5. sometimes—rises
6. Yesterday—read
7. first—produced
8. then—entered
9. commonly—wrote
10. still—use

EXERCISE B *(Answers will vary.)*
1. to what extent—really—had wanted
2. when—soon—built
3. how—carefully—painted
4. to what extent—partially—based
5. when—Never—had heard
6. when—Finally—arrived
7. how—quickly—arranged
8. how—well—went
9. how—loudly—applauded
10. when—soon—would create

WORKSHEET 7
Identifying Prepositions and Prepositional Phrases

EXERCISE A
1. of fire
2. by lightning
3. from this fire; in a shelter
4. within a cave
5. beside the coals
6. by these coals
7. of the fire
8. in the shelter
9. near the fire
10. during the Stone Age

EXERCISE B *(The first item is the preposition. The second is the object of the preposition.)*
1. under—rule; for—years
2. as—lawyer
3. through—means; for—independence
4. Because of—beliefs; with—nonviolence
5. with—it
6. of—nonviolence; for—truth
7. According to—Gandhi; of—strong
8. on—basis; of—people
9. of—disappointments; of—life; between—Hindus, Muslims; of—country
10. from—Great Britain

LANGUAGE HANDBOOK 1: THE PARTS OF SPEECH

WORKSHEET 8
Identifying Conjunctions and Interjections; Determining Parts of Speech

EXERCISE A
1. Whew; and
2. but
3. Neither, nor; and
4. Both, and
5. or
6. Hey, for
7. not only, but also
8. yet
9. but
10. Gosh, and

EXERCISE B
1. ADV
2. INT
3. ADJ
4. N
5. V
6. N
7. PREP
8. CONJ
9. ADJ
10. PRON

WORKSHEET 9
Test

EXERCISE A
1. mantis; is; insect; habits
2. creature; lives; parts; world
3. species; can be found; United States
4. mantis; is; friend; farmer
5. victims; include; grasshoppers; caterpillars
6. wait; prey; mantis; rests; legs
7. legs; captures; insects
8. mantis; does injure; plants
9. praying mantis; is used; greenhouses; control
10. praying mantis; may grow; inches; length

EXERCISE B
1. These; our
2. I; my; us; that; you
3. She; her; who
4. Your; most; himself; he; it
5. any; you; who
6. His; he; many
7. himself; whose; he
8. we; we; it; anyone; who
9. It; that; some; us
10. some; her; my; herself; it

EXERCISE C *(Answers in parentheses are considered optional.)*
1. early; readily; supernatural
2. long; predatory
3. female; many; frothy
4. This; eventually; (egg); tightly; woody
5. tall; very; common; (egg)
6. baby; soon; small; rapidly; out
7. newborn; often; immediately
8. adult; fierce
9. several; European; many; North American
10. These; Chinese; largest

EXERCISE D
1. to the library; about horses
2. by Toni Morrison; about the legacy; of slavery
3. across the country
4. Along the way; of Herbert Hoover; in West Branch, Iowa
5. beneath the sink; behind the cleanser
6. According to the newspaper; beside the river
7. Because of the heavy rains and flooding; through the city
8. in front of the house
9. near the garden
10. for his excellent films; among them

EXERCISE E
1. Gosh; and
2. either, or
3. Well; and; yet
4. but
5. Oops; neither, nor; but

EXERCISE F
1. PREP
2. N
3. V
4. PRON
5. ADJ
6. PREP
7. N
8. CONJ
9. ADV
10. INT

LANGUAGE HANDBOOK 2 AGREEMENT

WORKSHEET 1
Using Singular and Plural Forms

EXERCISE A
1. P
2. P
3. S
4. S
5. P
6. S
7. S
8. P
9. P
10. P
11. P
12. S
13. P
14. P
15. P
16. P
17. S
18. S
19. S
20. S
21. P
22. S
23. P
24. P
25. P

EXERCISE B
1. bottles
2. sheep
3. goats
4. apple
5. teams
6. I
7. noise
8. adenoids
9. galaxy
10. mountain lions

WORKSHEET 2
Making Subjects and Verbs Agree

EXERCISE A
1. sisters—enjoy
2. friends—have
3. members—are
4. You—turn
5. mail carrier—delivers
6. breeze—seems
7. people—do
8. robin—eats
9. We—were
10. They—call

EXERCISE B
1. work—consists
2. it—doesn't
3. No one—wants
4. tomatoes—have
5. garden—doesn't
6. you—weren't
7. newspapers—don't
8. uncle—comes
9. grandparents—were
10. Morning glories—close

WORKSHEET 3
Using Subjects and Verbs with Prepositional Phrases

EXERCISE A
1. descriptions (in the poem) (about Paul Revere) make
2. lines (in the poem) are
3. tramp (of feet) is
4. hoofbeats (of Paul Revere's horse) shatter
5. scenes (on each village street) live
6. poems (by Longfellow) have
7. One (of my favorite poems) is
8. antics (of the old man) make
9. Some (of the father's answers) (to his son) are
10. reason (for doing headstands) tickles

EXERCISE B
1. is
2. puts
3. moves
4. was
5. was
6. describe
7. takes
8. is
9. completes
10. seems

WORKSHEET 4
Ensuring Agreement with Indefinite Pronouns

EXERCISE A
1. needs
2. likes
3. prefer
4. cost
5. want
6. has
7. turn
8. becomes
9. has
10. were

EXERCISE B *(The first item in a pair is correct. The second is incorrect.)*
1. have—has
2. are—is
3. knows—know
4. are—is
5. wants—want
6. fear—fears
7. C
8. Do—Does
9. fill—fills
10. have—has

4 *Language Handbook Worksheets*

LANGUAGE HANDBOOK 2 AGREEMENT

WORKSHEET 5
Ensuring Agreement with Subjects Joined by *And, Or,* or *Nor*

EXERCISE A
1. La Tonya, Maria—play
2. Plot, character—are
3. Mosses, lichens—grow
4. president, owner—is
5. Apples, oranges, bananas—make
6. Country and western—has
7. *Little Women, Little Men*—were
8. Macaroni and cheese—is
9. Macaroni, cheese—are
10. pork—was

EXERCISE B
1. Li, Pang—reads
2. members, chairperson—was
3. jewelry, baskets—are
4. Jupiter, Zeus—Is
5. teacher, students—read
6. Tina, Fernando—likes
7. Channel 7, Channel 18—shows
8. Ms. Galinsky, Mr. Deneuve—has
9. Easter Island, Aleutian Islands—are
10. skiing, skiing—appeals

WORKSHEET 6
Ensuring Agreement with Collective Nouns and with *Don't* and *Doesn't*

EXERCISE A
1. is
2. is
3. are
4. have
5. talks
6. cheers
7. has
8. check
9. are
10. is

EXERCISE B
1. doesn't
2. don't
3. Doesn't
4. doesn't
5. don't
6. doesn't
7. Doesn't
8. don't
9. don't
10. doesn't

WORKSHEET 7
Ensuring Agreement in Questions and in Sentences That Begin with *There* and *Here*

EXERCISE
1. twirlers—come
2. students—are
3. members—Do
4. Miss Bannerman—does
5. references—are
6. Ms. Chang—Does
7. ice-skating—is
8. varieties—are
9. Amy—Has
10. receiver—was
11. everyone—Does
12. list—is
13. mistakes—are
14. truck—is
15. Drama Club—Isn't
16. Stephen—is
17. family—is
18. Emily Jones—Does
19. potholes—are
20. names—Have
21. attendance—Doesn't
22. Andres—Hasn't
23. one—is
24. boys—Were
25. several—are

WORKSHEET 8
Ensuring Agreement with Singular Words That Have Plural Forms

EXERCISE
1. comes
2. is
3. is
4. describes
5. meets
6. is
7. is
8. causes
9. is
10. is
11. is

Answer Key 5

LANGUAGE HANDBOOK 2 AGREEMENT

12. feels
13. is
14. is
15. helps
16. offers
17. is
18. equals
19. includes
20. is
21. seems
22. is
23. contains
24. was
25. makes

WORKSHEET 9
Ensuring Agreement Between Pronoun and Antecedent

EXERCISE

1. Dawna—she
2. Ramone, Ignacio—their
3. dog—his *or* its
4. Edgar Allan Poe—his
5. Everyone—his or her
6. book—its
7. Irwin Shapiro—him
8. dad—he
9. Many—they
10. No one—his or her
11. You—your
12. Paula—her
13. Janet—she
14. Virginia Driving Hawk Sneve—her
15. Any—your
16. I—my
17. rabbit—its
18. hikers—their
19. writer—her
20. Each—his
21. Shel Silverstein—his
22. Several—their
23. Each—his or her
24. ostrich—its
25. dogs, cat—their

WORKSHEET 10
Avoiding Problems in Agreement of Pronoun and Antecedent

EXERCISE

1. All—their
2. Andrea, Estrella—her
3. Most—their
4. Everybody—his or her
5. Anyone—his or her
6. Several—their
7. Nobody—his or her
8. Each—her
9. Someone—his
10. Everyone—his or her
11. Most—their
12. few—their
13. somebody—his or her
14. either—him
15. Many—their
16. any—their
17. No one—his or her
18. anybody—his or her
19. Some—their
20. None—its
21. Both—their
22. Most—its
23. One—her
24. None—their
25. Neither—its

WORKSHEET 11
Ensuring Pronoun-Antecedent Agreement with *And, Or,* and *Nor*

EXERCISE A

1. his
2. their
3. their
4. her
5. their
6. her
7. their
8. his
9. their
10. her
11. its
12. they
13. its
14. he
15. they
16. his
17. their
18. his
19. they
20. she

6 Language Handbook Worksheets

LANGUAGE HANDBOOK 2 AGREEMENT

EXERCISE B *(Revisions may vary.)*
1. Either Jennifer will be bringing her catcher's mitt to the softball game, or Walter will be bringing his.
2. Either Joseph will surprise us with his special recipe at the dinner party, or the Wongs will surprise us with theirs.
3. Both Christopher and Louise failed to submit their stories to the student newspaper.
4. I suppose that both Clancy and the Donovans will be unwilling to give us their accounts of what happened.

WORKSHEET 12
Avoiding Problems in Agreement of Pronoun and Antecedent

EXERCISE
1. swarm—its
2. (two) miles—it
3. committee—its
4. news—it
5. group—their
6. family—its
7. Congress—their
8. flock—its
9. (two) quarts—its
10. *Idylls of the King*—its
11. herd—their
12. jury—its
13. (sixty-three) cents—it
14. assembly—their
15. Physics—it
16. (ten) pounds—it
17. civics—it
18. public—their
19. committee—its
20. Measles—it
21. team—its
22. orchestra—their
23. staff—their
24. (ten) miles—it
25. class—its

WORKSHEET 13
Test

EXERCISE A
1. S
2. P
3. P
4. S
5. P
6. S
7. S
8. P
9. P
10. S

EXERCISE B
1. There are
2. is
3. doesn't
4. are
5. was
6. was
7. seems
8. hope
9. has
10. don't
11. don't
12. Do
13. sell
14. boards
15. retrieve
16. were
17. is
18. come
19. weren't
20. aren't

EXERCISE C *(The first item in a set is the correct verb. The second item is the subject. The third item is the incorrect verb.)*
1. were—effects—was
2. were—swimmers—was
3. are—recipes—is
4. C—beauty
5. has—Each—have
6. C—Towns, seaports
7. was—tale—were
8. C—One
9. C—explorations, adventures
10. is—Trade—are

EXERCISE D
1. None—have
2. Lions Club—meets
3. Lola, Sam—plan
4. (Twenty) pounds—is
5. Mathematics—is
6. writer, director—was
7. Most—was
8. (Two-and-a-half) months—is
9. "Points of View"—is
10. news—is

Answer Key **7**

LANGUAGE HANDBOOK 2 AGREEMENT

EXERCISE E
1. has
2. live
3. have
4. are
5. is
6. reads
7. Do
8. take
9. is
10. come

EXERCISE F
1. LaTonya, Darlene—her
2. band, choir—they
3. some—their
4. (ten) dollars—it
5. team—its
6. animal—its
7. economics—it
8. All—their
9. Everyone—his or her
10. "Peter and the Wolf"—it

LANGUAGE HANDBOOK 3 USING VERBS

WORKSHEET 1
Identifying Past, Present, and Future Tenses

EXERCISE A
1. believe; (have) believed
2. shouted; (have) shouted
3. asking; (have) asked
4. liked; (have) liked
5. climb; climbing
6. work; worked
7. smile; smiled
8. following; (have) followed
9. support; supporting
10. complete; completed

EXERCISE B
1. sponsoring
2. listened
3. switched
4. removed
5. switching
6. changed
7. closed
8. gaining
9. purchasing
10. achieved

WORKSHEET 2
Using Irregular Verbs

EXERCISE
1. did
2. put
3. gone
4. took
5. begun
6. saw
7. read
8. lent
9. made
10. come
11. hurt
12. broken
13. taught
14. kept
15. ate
16. found
17. drank
18. spread
19. knew
20. burst
21. sent
22. rang
23. drove
24. become
25. shook

WORKSHEET 3
More Practice with Irregular Verbs

EXERCISE A
1. taken
2. made
3. shot
4. found
5. begun
6. held
7. spoken
8. written
9. thrown
10. knew
11. taught
12. driven
13. flown
14. ran
15. swam
16. brought
17. chosen
18. drank
19. known
20. threw
21. frozen
22. swum
23. broken
24. thought
25. began

EXERCISE B
1. done
2. have come
3. seen
4. went
5. come
6. done
7. came
8. saw
9. gone
10. come

EXERCISE C
1. brought
2. C
3. drank
4. swum
5. ridden
6. run
7. driven
8. ridden
9. knew
10. C

WORKSHEET 4
Identifying and Using Verb Tenses

EXERCISE A
1. past
2. future perfect
3. present perfect
4. future
5. past perfect
6. past
7. present
8. present perfect
9. future perfect
10. past perfect

Answer Key **9**

LANGUAGE HANDBOOK 3: USING VERBS

EXERCISE B

1. The band plays the same songs at every game.
2. We had seen several whales as we cruised beyond the waters of the bay.
3. Andrea demonstrated the proper way to fold the flag.
4. The butterflies will have migrated to Mexico by the end of fall.
5. Mr. Sharp has shown us how to block a scene in theater class today.
6. The rancher will explain to us the difference between an emu and an ostrich.
7. Ahmed has taken his brother home by now.
8. Many divers knew about Jacob's Well for years.
9. We will have begun our tour of British Columbia after visiting Seattle.
10. The students had handed in their homework.

WORKSHEET 5
Using Consistent Verb Tense

EXERCISE A *(Here is the paragraph in present tense.)*

[1] By the time Saturday comes, I am ready to go. [2] Jeff's parents drive us there, and we park as close to the front entrance as we can. [3] After making arrangements to meet them in two hours at the bumper cars, we walk down the midway. [4] There are all kinds of rides, and we decide which ones we want to try. [5] We find a ticket booth, and we each buy twelve tickets. [6] For the first ride, we take it easy and just go on the Ferris wheel. [7] It's fun to see all the lights when we are stopped at the top of the wheel. [8] After that, we go on a couple of wild rides that are scary but fun. [9] All that excitement makes us thirsty, so we find a refreshment stand and order two lemonades. [10] Before we know it, it is ten o'clock and time to meet Jeff's parents.

(Here is the paragraph in past tense.)

[1] By the time Saturday came, I was ready to go. [2] Jeff's parents drove us there, and we parked as close to the front entrance as we could. [3] After making arrangements to meet them in two hours at the bumper cars, we walked down the midway. [4] There were all kinds of rides, and we decided which ones we wanted to try. [5] We found a ticket booth, and we each bought twelve tickets. [6] For the first ride, we took it easy and just went on the Ferris wheel. [7] It was fun to see all the lights when we were stopped at the top of the wheel. [8] After that, we went on a couple of wild rides that were scary but fun. [9] All that excitement made us thirsty, so we found a refreshment stand and ordered two lemonades. [10] Before we knew it, it was ten o'clock and time to meet Jeff's parents.

EXERCISE B *(Here is the paragraph in present tense.)*

[1] Eleanor Roosevelt's parents die when she is nine, so she is raised by her grandmother and sent to school in England. [2] There, she is influenced by headmistress Marie Souvestre, who works for social causes. [3] As a young adult, Eleanor participates in social work before she marries Franklin Delano Roosevelt. [4] After her husband enters politics, she works for the American Red Cross during World War I and later becomes more involved in politics herself. [5] In the early 1930s, Mrs. Roosevelt becomes a leading activist for women's rights. [6] When her husband is elected President of the United States, Mrs. Roosevelt helps other women get appointed to government positions. [7] She travels around the country, visits coal mines and slums, and speaks out for the poor. [8] After her husband's death, Mrs. Roosevelt is appointed by President Truman to be a delegate to the United Nations, where she supports the UN's Declaration of Human Rights. [9] This service in the UN is probably her greatest achievement. [10] Eleanor Roosevelt devotes herself to the causes of humanity and is loved by many.

(Here is the paragraph in past tense.)

[1] Eleanor Roosevelt's parents died when she was nine, so she was raised by her grandmother and sent to school in England. [2] There, she was influenced by headmistress Marie Souvestre, who worked for social causes. [3] As a young adult, Eleanor participated in social work before she married Franklin Delano Roosevelt. [4] After her husband entered politics, she worked for the American Red Cross during World War I and later became more involved in politics herself. [5] In the early 1930s, Mrs. Roosevelt became a leading activist for women's rights. [6] When her husband was elected President of the United States, Mrs. Roosevelt helped other women get appointed to government positions. [7] She traveled around the country, visited coal mines and slums, and spoke out for the poor. [8] After her husband's death, Mrs. Roosevelt was appointed by President Truman to be

LANGUAGE HANDBOOK 3: USING VERBS

a delegate to the United Nations, where she supported the UN's Declaration of Human Rights. [9] This service in the UN was probably her greatest achievement. [10] Eleanor Roosevelt devoted herself to the causes of humanity and was loved by many.

WORKSHEET 6
Identifying and Using Active and Passive Voice

EXERCISE A
1. AV
2. PV
3. PV
4. AV
5. PV
6. PV
7. PV
8. AV
9. AV
10. PV

EXERCISE B *(Word order in revisions may vary slightly.)*
1. A lasagna dinner was cooked for the family last night by Dad.
2. Several members of our foreign cultures club attended the folk-dancing class.
3. Some friends were invited by Sarah to go to the movies with her on Saturday.
4. Many people see famous works of art in the Louvre Museum in Paris.
5. A professional tree trimmer pruned our pecan tree.
6. A slide show and lecture on native plants of the Southwest was given by Glen.
7. The students read Lincoln's Gettysburg Address.
8. I was invited by the Hardens to their annual Labor Day picnic.
9. Dr. Lambert gave our dog his rabies vaccination.
10. A technician fixed our computer.

WORKSHEET 7
Using *Sit* and *Set*

EXERCISE A
1. sitting
2. set
3. sitting
4. sat
5. set
6. sat
7. sitting
8. set
9. sit
10. set

EXERCISE B
1. sit
2. set
3. sit
4. setting
5. sets
6. sits
7. setting
8. sitting
9. Set
10. sits

WORKSHEET 8
Using *Lie* and *Lay*

EXERCISE A
1. lying
2. lay
3. lay
4. lay
5. lying
6. lain
7. laying
8. laid
9. laid
10. lie

EXERCISE B
1. lying
2. lie
3. lay
4. lay
5. laid
6. lain
7. laid
8. lay
9. lie
10. lay

WORKSHEET 9
Using *Rise* and *Raise*

EXERCISE A
1. rose
2. raise
3. rose
4. raise
5. raised
6. rose
7. rise
8. raise
9. rises
10. raise

EXERCISE B
1. rising
2. rose
3. raising
4. raise
5. risen
6. raised (*or* raises)
7. rose (*or* rises)
8. raised
9. rose
10. rises

Answer Key 11

LANGUAGE HANDBOOK 3 USING VERBS

WORKSHEET 10

Test

EXERCISE A
1. returned
2. shouting
3. use
4. wipe
5. like
6. worked
7. completing
8. smiled
9. asked
10. supporting

EXERCISE B
1. saw
2. chosen
3. led
4. spread
5. got
6. Did
7. made
8. eaten
9. begun
10. brought

EXERCISE C
1. had broken
2. has sung
3. will have finished
4. has worked
5. empties; feeds
6. will design; will market
7. passed
8. went
9. has played
10. flew

EXERCISE D *(Here is the paragraph in present tense.)*

[1] "Casey at the Bat," composed by Ernest Lawrence Thayer in 1888, becomes the most famous baseball poem ever written. [2] The poem is recited around the country, and audiences love it. [3] However, Thayer considers the poem badly written and for years does not admit he is the author. [4] Many people try to take credit for the poem, and several baseball players say the poem is about them. [5] When the author is finally identified, he refuses to take money for the poem's many reprintings.

(Here is the paragraph in past tense.)

[1] "Casey at the Bat," composed by Ernest Lawrence Thayer in 1888, became the most famous baseball poem ever written. [2] The poem was recited around the country, and audiences loved it. [3] However, Thayer considered the poem badly written and for years did not admit he was the author. [4] Many people tried to take credit for the poem, and several baseball players said the poem was about them. [5] When the author was finally identified, he refused to take money for the poem's many reprintings.

EXERCISE E
1. AV
2. PV
3. PV
4. AV
5. PV

EXERCISE F
1. laid
2. raise
3. sits
4. lying
5. rose
6. lying
7. set
8. laid
9. lies
10. risen

LANGUAGE HANDBOOK 4 USING PRONOUNS

WORKSHEET 1
Identifying and Using Pronouns in the Nominative Case

EXERCISE

1. She	14. they
2. We	15. we
3. It	16. They
4. they	17. she
5. We	18. it
6. He	19. they
7. they	20. He
8. They	21. they
9. she	22. she
10. They	23. they
11. she	24. he
12. he	25. you
13. They	

WORKSHEET 2
Identifying and Using Pronouns as Predicate Nominatives

EXERCISE A

1. she	6. she
2. they	7. I
3. he	8. he; we
4. they	9. he
5. she	10. we

EXERCISE B *(The first item in a pair is correct. The second is incorrect.)*

1. C	6. he—him
2. she—her	7. C
3. we—us	8. we—us
4. C	9. he—him
5. I—me	10. I—me

WORKSHEET 3
Using Pronouns as Direct Objects

EXERCISE

1. me	14. her
2. them	15. her
3. them	16. us
4. us	17. him
5. him	18. her; me
6. her	19. them; me
7. him	20. her
8. him; her	21. me
9. me	22. us
10. her	23. me
11. him	24. them
12. us	25. us
13. them; me	

WORKSHEET 4
Using Pronouns in the Objective Case

EXERCISE

1. us	14. them
2. them	15. me
3. them	16. me
4. us	17. her
5. him or her	18. her
6. us	19. them
7. us	20. me
8. us	21. them
9. him or her	22. us
10. us	23. her
11. them	24. us
12. them	25. me
13. us	

Answer Key **13**

LANGUAGE HANDBOOK 4 USING PRONOUNS

WORKSHEET 5
Using Pronouns as Objects of Prepositions

EXERCISE
1. me
2. her
3. her
4. me
5. him
6. them
7. us
8. him; her
9. them; me
10. him
11. me
12. him
13. us
14. me
15. her
16. him; me
17. him
18. her; him
19. them
20. us
21. him
22. us
23. her
24. him
25. her

WORKSHEET 6
Using *Who* and *Whom* and Reflexive Pronouns

EXERCISE A
1. whom
2. Whom
3. who
4. whom
5. who
6. whom
7. who
8. who
9. Who
10. who

EXERCISE B
1. themselves
2. myself
3. I
4. himself
5. themselves
6. I
7. myself
8. yourselves
9. me
10. himself

WORKSHEET 7
More Practice with Pronouns

EXERCISE A
1. us
2. We
3. us
4. us
5. us
6. us
7. We
8. us
9. us
10. We

EXERCISE B
1. whom
2. who
3. we
4. themselves
5. we
6. me
7. whom
8. I
9. who
10. themselves

WORKSHEET 8
Test

EXERCISE A
1. who
2. he
3. she
4. me
5. We
6. who
7. they
8. she
9. me
10. yourself

EXERCISE B
1. OP
2. PRED NOM
3. SUBJ
4. DO
5. SUBJ
6. SUBJ
7. SUBJ
8. OP
9. SUBJ
10. DO

EXERCISE C
1. I
2. me
3. he
4. her
5. them
6. her
7. us
8. her
9. we
10. they

EXERCISE D (*The first item in a pair is correct. The second is incorrect.*)
1. me—I
2. We—Us
3. C
4. me—I
5. him—he

EXERCISE E
1. themselves
2. himself
3. We
4. Who
5. us
6. yourself
7. whom
8. me
9. her
10. who

14 *Language Handbook Worksheets*

LANGUAGE HANDBOOK 4 USING PRONOUNS

EXERCISE F *(The first item in a pair is correct. The second is incorrect.)*
1. me—I
2. C
3. him—he
4. C
5. them—they
6. us—we
7. him—he
8. me—I
9. C
10. C

Answer Key **15**

LANGUAGE HANDBOOK 5: USING MODIFIERS

WORKSHEET 1
Identifying and Using Modifiers in Regular and Irregular Comparisons

EXERCISE A
1. farther
2. more intriguing
3. most distant
4. closer
5. stranger
6. best
7. harder
8. most respected
9. better
10. most

EXERCISE B
1. superlative
2. comparative
3. positive
4. comparative
5. comparative
6. superlative
7. superlative
8. comparative
9. positive
10. superlative

WORKSHEET 2
Using Modifiers Correctly

EXERCISE A
1. worst
2. better
3. most famous
4. more
5. more curious
6. less
7. most important
8. heaviest
9. worse
10. better

EXERCISE B
1. largest
2. deeper
3. stronger
4. newer
5. more snugly
6. most gigantic
7. most interesting
8. good
9. better
10. highest

WORKSHEET 3
Using *Other* and *Else;* Avoiding Double Comparisons and Double Negatives

EXERCISE A (The first item in a pair is standard. The second is nonstandard.)
1. any other story—any story
2. anyone else in the studio—anyone in the studio
3. any other kind—any kind
4. anyone else—anyone
5. any other time—any time
6. anyone else—anyone
7. any other writer—any writer
8. anything else—anything
9. any other character—any character
10. any other writer—any writer

EXERCISE B (The first item in a pair is correct. The second is incorrect.)
1. can be no *or* can't be any—can't be no
2. more ready *or* readier—more readier
3. won't ever guess *or* will never guess—won't never guess
4. can hardly wait *or* can't wait—can't hardly wait
5. odder—more odder
6. couldn't find ... anywhere *or* could find ... nowhere—couldn't find ... nowhere
7. quieter *or* more quiet—more quieter
8. could scarcely *or* couldn't—couldn't scarcely
9. the funniest *or* most funny—the most funniest
10. Nobody had ever—Nobody had never

WORKSHEET 4
Correcting Misplaced Modifiers

EXERCISE (Revisions may vary slightly.)
1. Hoping for a chance to play for the all-stars, he would pitch his final ballgame tonight.
2. That morning he had promised himself he would not be nervous at the game.
3. Donnie's sandwich that he had made the night before tasted good.
4. Trying not to think about the game, he looked up at the birds in the tree.
5. He noticed a male cardinal looking back at him.
6. The brilliant red bird on the limb seemed to tilt his head toward Donnie.
7. Leaning against the trunk, Donnie looked for a nest.
8. Finding no signs of other birds, he was puzzled by the presence of the cardinal.
9. Then, from the corner of his eye, he could see the bird's beak open.
10. C
11. C
12. As they approached, they asked him if he was going to pitch a no-hitter.
13. Finishing his sandwich, he joked that he was going to walk all the batters.
14. Without mentioning the bird, Donnie suggested they head for the cafeteria.

16 Language Handbook Worksheets

LANGUAGE HANDBOOK 5 USING MODIFIERS

15. Even through his afternoon classes, however, the bird in the tree came to mind.
16. That night, growing less worried about the outcome of the game, Donnie dressed in the locker room among his teammates.
17. C
18. C
19. There was no way of predicting how a final decision on the all-stars would turn out.
20. Still, Donnie, wearing a bright red cap, felt lucky walking out on the field.

WORKSHEET 5
Correcting Dangling and Misplaced Modifiers

EXERCISE *(Revisions will vary.)*

1. Wanting to get rich quickly, some men thought of a plan to kidnap a boy.
2. Kicking and fighting, the boy caused nothing but trouble.
3. Whining hungrily, the child was quickly served dinner.
4. Having finally dozed off, one kidnapper was awakened at daybreak by screams.
5. Terrified and humiliated, the other man had been surprised by the boy's attack.
6. Fearing the parents wouldn't pay, the kidnappers began to see their plan as less wise.
7. Who wouldn't want a vacation from the boy who pestered and threatened everyone?
8. Going on his way to collect the ransom, the kidnapper isn't sure what he will find.
9. You expect O. Henry's story, using exaggeration and irony, to get funnier.
10. Not wanting to spoil the surprise, I will keep the conclusion secret.
11. If you are familiar with O. Henry, you expect an ending with a twist.
12. Because O. Henry uses irony to create humor, his stories are filled with contrast.
13. Filled with colorful characters, O. Henry's stories describe his and others' experiences.
14. When he describes victims of fate, his characters have tragic and lonely lives.
15. The underworld life was a source of material for the many stories he wrote in prison.
16. In spite of a short and tragic life, O. Henry wrote stories that were often humorous.
17. You may appreciate O. Henry's style, which is marked by a little sadness mixed with humor.
18. Because I am interested in humorous writers, their biographies fascinate me.
19. If you want to find a collection of his work, the library is a good place to start.
20. After you check the table of contents, several titles may look familiar.

WORKSHEET 6
Test

EXERCISE A
1. most familiar
2. any other
3. more secure
4. can hardly
5. longest
6. anyone else
7. will never
8. less dense
9. any
10. better

EXERCISE B
1. Balancing on the high dive
2. Without blaming anyone
3. C
4. after next semester
5. with red hair
6. as he daydreamed
7. on both sides of the state line
8. C
9. C
10. Looking up

EXERCISE C
1. higher
2. most stupendous
3. best
4. any other
5. bluer
6. could hardly
7. any other
8. more beautiful
9. ever
10. anyone else

EXERCISE D
1. I
2. I
3. I
4. I
5. C
6. I
7. C
8. I
9. C
10. C

Answer Key **17**

LANGUAGE HANDBOOK 6 PHRASES

WORKSHEET 1
Identifying Prepositional Phrases

EXERCISE A
1. PHR
2. PHR
3. NP
4. PHR
5. NP
6. PHR
7. PHR
8. NP
9. PHR
10. PHR

EXERCISE B
1. about the Columbia River
2. in the Canadian Rocky Mountains
3. of this mighty river
4. at The Dalles
5. near the Columbia River
6. During the Ice Age
7. of the Columbia
8. through the Grand Coulee region
9. to the Grand Coulee Dam
10. in Washington

WORKSHEET 2
Identifying and Using Adjective Phrases

EXERCISE A (The first item in a pair is the adjective phrase. The second is the word modified.)
1. from the Dominican Republic—singer
2. NONE
3. of two popular Caribbean styles, salsa and merengue—blend
4. about social issues in the Dominican Republic and Latin America—lyrics; in the Dominican Republic and Latin America—issues
5. of other Caribbean and African styles of music—roots; of music—styles
6. in Santo Domingo, the capital of the Dominican Republic—neighborhood; of the Dominican Republic—capital
7. in Boston, Massachusetts—college
8. of his albums—One

EXERCISE B (Sentences will vary.)
1. My sister gave her new scarf to someone in her class.
2. He is an author with a distinctive style.
3. The map under the chair is the one we need.
4. On a clear night I like to look up and see the stars above me.
5. Each of you will get your chance.

WORKSHEET 3
Identifying and Using Adverb Phrases

EXERCISE A (The first item in a pair is the adverb phrase. The second is the word or words modified.)
1. on the first Monday in September—is celebrated
2. NONE
3. in the United States—initiated
4. In 1882—held; in New York City—held
5. on the first Monday in September—held
6. in other states—campaigned
7. During the next few years—was passed; in four states—was passed
8. In 1894—declared
9. with parades and speeches by labor leaders and political figures—is celebrated

EXERCISE B (Sentences will vary.)
1. I spent the whole weekend without leaving home.
2. They waited in the emergency room for more than two hours.
3. According to the teacher the test results will be here on Monday.
4. The parade should start around ten o'clock.
5. My great-great-grandfather came to the United States from England during the last century.

WORKSHEET 4
Identifying Present and Past Participles and Participial Phrases

EXERCISE A (The first item in a pair is the present participle or participial phrase. The second is the word or words modified.)
1. growing—popularity
2. Peacefully floating on the lake—Rob, Lucio
3. NONE
4. braying—donkey
5. eagerly expecting a letter from his best friend—Ahmed
6. NONE
7. Wanting to commemorate the primates at the Philadelphia Zoo—artist

18 Language Handbook Worksheets

LANGUAGE HANDBOOK 6 PHRASES

8. changing—colors
9. NONE
10. Studying French literature—sister

EXERCISE B *(The first item in a pair is the past participle or participial phrase. The second is the word or words modified.)*

1. Born in New Orleans in 1961—Wynton Marsalis
2. Soundly defeated—soldiers
3. NONE
4. wounded—pride
5. unanswered—letter
6. broken and forgotten—tractor
7. located in Southeast Asia—Myanmar
8. NONE
9. written in German—contract
10. Now also cultivated in the United States—fruit
11. encouraged by the audience's applause—Heidi
12. Ashamed of his rudeness to his mother's visitor—Rudy
13. completely exhausted by his twelve-hour day in the field—farmer
14. surprised—burglar
15. NONE
16. frustrated—two-year-old
17. sidelined by a torn ligament—player
18. Elected by a large margin—politician
19. NONE
20. Overwhelmed by a crush of hungry diners—owner
21. enraged—steer
22. Accompanied by John on drums, Luther on bass, and Travis on guitar—Kenny
23. struck by lightning—transformer
24. lined—face
25. pierced—lantern

WORKSHEET 5
Identifying and Using Gerunds and Gerund Phrases

EXERCISE A
1. NONE
2. Listening to this amazing recording
3. doing a little research at the library
4. NONE
5. celebrating community and personal events
6. Singing
7. making music
8. adding a voice or a clap pattern to a song's chorus
9. the performing of special songs
10. group singing; clearing thick brush for rice fields

EXERCISE B
1. NONE
2. DO—low chanting
3. PN—repairing the wicker on chairs.
4. S—Living in San Diego
5. OP—studying for four hours

WORKSHEET 6
Identifying and Using Infinitives and Infinitive Phrases

EXERCISE A
1. to complete for tomorrow
2. to listen to Tonya reading poetry
3. to play with his grandson all day.
4. To get to the theater on time
5. NONE

EXERCISE B
1. N—to compete in sled dog racing
2. N—to win the Iditarod Trail Sled Dog Race four times
3. ADV—to become involved in sled dog racing, or mushing
4. ADV—to train a dog team
5. N—To race in the Iditarod
6. N—to lead a sled dog team to the summit of Mount McKinley for the first time
7. ADV—to accomplish that dream
8. N—to withdraw her team from the Iditarod because of a moose attack
9. ADJ—to win the race
10. N—To win the famous race even once

WORKSHEET 7
Identifying and Using Appositives and Appositive Phrases

EXERCISE A
1. a machine tool used for cutting metal or wood
2. the language of the Incas
3. George Gershwin; *Porgy and Bess*
4. a scientist and science fiction writer
5. NONE

Answer Key **19**

LANGUAGE HANDBOOK 6 PHRASES

EXERCISE B *(The first item in a pair is the appositive or appositive phrase. The second is the word or words the appositive or appositive phrase explains or identifies.)*

1. HDTV—High-definition television
2. the Roman philosopher and statesman—Seneca
3. A four-time recipient of the Pulitzer Prize for poetry—Robert Frost
4. both Romance languages—French, Spanish
5. Sandra's favorite painter—Caravaggio
6. corn and potatoes—crops
7. Osaka, Kyoto, and Nagasaki—cities
8. Robert's cousin—Lucy Telotte
9. the domestic dog—*Canis familiaris*
10. Ingrid—friend

WORKSHEET 8

Test

EXERCISE A *(The first item in a pair is the prepositional phrase. The second is the word or words modified.)*

1. of rain—droplets; outside the house—were falling
2. from the locker room—came; to their bus—went
3. around the lake—road; after the heavy rains—was flooded
4. about a boy and his dog—tells
5. of the dog—name; in the novel—dog
6. of rice—bag; in the cupboard—Did find; in the pantry—Did find
7. from the car—bring; on the kitchen table—set
8. Over the trees—saw
9. by the author Langston Hughes—anything
10. up the hill—neighbors; of ours—friends

EXERCISE B *(The first item in a pair is the word or words modified. The second is the participle or participial phrase.)*

1. collar—newly purchased
2. face—smiling
3. technicians—Trained
4. cat—stalking the bird in the back yard
5. features—most recommended
6. Moira—Going through her backpack
7. sister—wearing a wool cap
8. statues—strikingly carved
9. fire—burning in the large fireplace
10. hurricane—fed by cool wind currents and warm sea water

EXERCISE C

1. S—Piloting twin-rotor helicopters
2. DO—watching travel videos
3. OP—winning civil rights for African Americans
4. DO—your windsurfing
5. S—The senator's thinking on the issues
6. PN—constructing Stonehenge
7. PN—ice-skating
8. DO—keeping pigeons
9. S—the rumbling of the railroad car
10. S—Revealing the ending of the book

EXERCISE D

1. N—to be there early
2. ADV—to have rescued the cat from the burning house
3. ADV—To fill the swimming pool
4. N—to boil the water before putting in the pasta
5. N—To sing the role of Mimi in *La Bohème* at the Metropolitan Opera
6. ADJ—to decorate the gym for the dance
7. N—to ride his bicycle to the farmer's market
8. ADJ—to write their advertisements for them
9. ADV—to hear the result of the composer's revisions to the concerto
10. ADV—to score a touchdown

EXERCISE E *(The first item in a pair is the word or words identified or explained by the appositive or appositive phrase. The second item is the appositive or appositive phrase.)*

1. dog—a Labrador retriever
2. B-52—a jet bomber
3. book—*Moby-Dick*
4. cat—Thomasina
5. Colossus of Rhodes—one of the Seven Wonders of the Ancient World
6. grandfather—a Lakota medicine man
7. Galileo Galilei—the Italian astronomer
8. brother—Mike
9. Seder—a feast to celebrate the flight of the Jews from slavery in Egypt
10. Toni Morrison—a Nobel Prize-winning author

LANGUAGE HANDBOOK 7: CLAUSES

WORKSHEET 1
Identifying Independent and Subordinate Clauses

EXERCISE A
1. IND—Today ... birthday.
2. SUB
3. IND—On ... *Limber Lost.*
4. IND—He ... Montana.
5. SUB
6. IND—Reluctantly ... back.
7. SUB
8. SUB
9. IND—We ... canoe.
10. SUB

EXERCISE B
1. After the rain stopped; that she thought were very dirty
2. where a dirty car was parked out front
3. Because she is a good salesperson; whom she approached
4. as she washed their station wagon
5. that she washed and waxed
6. NONE
7. that she earned; which distributes funds to flood victims
8. That her money is going toward a good cause

WORKSHEET 2
Identifying and Using Adjective Clauses

EXERCISE A *(The first item in a pair is the adjective clause. The second is the word modified.)*
1. which includes thirty-one paintings—series
2. who underwent incredible struggles—persons
3. that may have been overlooked—scenes
4. which include bold images and vivid colors—techniques
5. who was a former slave—Tubman
6. which show both slavery and freedom—scenes
7. that reflect slavery—images
8. whose paintings were probably influenced by others' descriptions—Lawrence
9. that advertises a reward for Tubman's capture—caption
10. which brought an end to slavery—Civil War

EXERCISE B
1. We read The Autobiography of Miss Jane Pittman, which is about an African American woman reflecting on her life.
2. Ronald has a new car that has air conditioning.
3. Mrs. Olson, who owns a grocery store on Park Street, contributed some canned food for our food drive.
4. Here is an Ernesto Galarza story that I found in a book in my grandparents' attic.
5. Yolanda, whose voice is lovely, is the star of our musical.

EXERCISE C
1. who (*or* that)
2. that (*or* which)
3. whom
4. whose
5. who (*or* that)
6. that (*or* which)
7. who (*or* that)
8. whom
9. which (*or* that)
10. which (*or* that)

WORKSHEET 3
Identifying and Using Adverb Clauses

EXERCISE A
1. <u>because</u> they can practice it year-round
2. <u>before</u> they go to school
3. <u>so that</u> she can be the best in that event
4. <u>since</u> it develops his shoulder and arm muscles
5. <u>whenever</u> they are held in the area
6. <u>If</u> they practice
7. <u>as</u> they practice
8. <u>after</u> each meet is over
9. <u>Although</u> swimming is usually an individual sport
10. <u>As soon as</u> Maria's younger sister is old enough to compete

EXERCISE B *(Order of clauses will vary.)*
1. Because Mother's birthday is tomorrow, Luis is going to prepare a special dinner.
2. Amy prepared the salad while we stripped the husks off the corn.
3. I can't go to the game since I must finish my science notebook.
4. After my pen ran out of ink, I finished my outline in pencil.
5. Although I knew I was going to do well, I worried about the history test.

Answer Key 21

LANGUAGE HANDBOOK 7 CLAUSES

6. When we were hunting for project material, we found three articles on the Battle of Wounded Knee.
7. Although Jill was the smallest girl on her team, she was the best player.
8. Since Brian has overslept, he will be late for school.
9. We gave up our picnic plans because the rain was beginning to fall.
10. After Mom and Dad had left for the political caucus, Lisa and I began our homework.

WORKSHEET 4
Identifying Noun Clauses

EXERCISE A
1. what we would like to do as a community volunteer project
2. whoever does it
3. That we give help to more than one person
4. what really needs to be done
5. what Lacreesha had suggested

EXERCISE B
1. S—Whoever knows me
2. OP—whatever game is on TV at the moment
3. PN—what fascinates me the most
4. NONE
5. S—That Olajuwon was voted NBA Defensive Player of the Year in 1994
6. OP—what he does best: blocking shots, rebounding, and scoring
7. DO—that Olajuwon wrote an autobiography, *Living the Dream: My Life and Basketball*
8. IO—whoever watched him on the court
9. S—That Abdul-Jabbar led the Los Angeles Lakers to five NBA championships
10. PN—that he changed his name from Lew Alcindor in 1971

WORKSHEET 5
Test

EXERCISE A
1. SUB
2. IND
3. SUB
4. IND
5. SUB
6. IND
7. SUB
8. SUB
9. IND
10. SUB

EXERCISE B
1. which is a popular Basque handball game
2. who also wrote detective stories
3. that I want
4. that we are playing in the Thanksgiving program
5. whose photographs are on display
6. that Yo-Yo Ma has played since the age of four
7. whom many remember as the author of *Frankenstein*
8. that are often used in electronic components
9. who headed for California during the gold rush
10. which was in an accident

EXERCISE C
1. Because she works long hours at her new office
2. since he comes home first
3. Although he had cooked at cookouts and on Sunday mornings
4. because he is willing to experiment
5. because he finds them tasty
6. when he was a foreign correspondent in Thailand
7. If Mother, Father, and I all pitch in and clean up after dinner
8. since Mother started her job
9. after we have cleaned up from dinner
10. so that we can take a trip to South America this summer

22 *Language Handbook Worksheets*

LANGUAGE HANDBOOK 8 SENTENCES

WORKSHEET 1
Identifying Sentences and Sentence Fragments

EXERCISE

1. F
2. S—Kevin has several rods and reels.
3. S—The bluefish start running in the late summer.
4. F
5. S—They require big hooks and a strong fishing rod.
6. F
7. S—They breed in freshwater rivers.
8. F
9. F
10. S—Don't party boats take many people to the fishing grounds?
11. S—Flounder can be found in coves.
12. S—Pull your hook up a couple of inches from the bottom.
13. F
14. S—Are all fish good to eat?
15. S—Menhaden are caught for fertilizer.
16. F
17. F
18. S—Sandworms make very good bait.
19. S—A funny-looking fish is the sea robin.
20. S—It swells up to twice its size when caught.
21. S—Is it designed to frighten its enemies?
22. F
23. S—One time Kevin caught an eel.
24. F
25. F

WORKSHEET 2
Correcting Sentence Fragments

EXERCISE *(If students have not yet studied comma usage, do not grade for comma placement.)*

1. F—The Cherokee constructed their towns in fortified places in the mountains. So that they could live in peace, isolated from aggressive neighbors.
2. F—When the settlers moved into their lands, the Cherokee tried to adapt to the new culture.
3. F—Under the leadership of Chief Sequoyah, they drew up a constitution for their nation, following the example of the settlers.
4. F—Many of the new settlers did not want to live side by side with the Cherokee, whom they considered a conquered nation.
5. F—In 1802, the federal government, promising land in the Great Plains, agreed to move the Cherokee from Georgia.
6. F—The Cherokee tried to obtain justice and brought suit against Georgia in a case called *Cherokee Nation* v. *Georgia,* 1831.
7. S
8. F—It seemed like a victory, but President Andrew Jackson refused to intervene when Georgia denied the Cherokee their rights.
9. F—The Cherokee were forced to leave their ancestral home in favor of lands promised them in the Great Plains.
10. S

WORKSHEET 3
Identifying the Complete Subject and the Complete Predicate

EXERCISE

1. <u>Maritza's favorite things to draw</u> <u>are imaginary creatures</u>.
2. <u>She and her friends</u> <u>spend hours inventing beasts</u>.
3. Then <u>they</u> <u>vote for the most imaginative creature among the group</u>.
4. Can <u>you</u> <u>guess Maritza's favorite fabulous creature</u>?
5. <u>It</u> <u>is the legendary monster called the griffin</u>.
6. <u>The griffin</u> <u>is a combination of species</u>.
7. <u>Having the head, beak, and wings of an eagle and the body and legs of a lion, the griffin</u> <u>represents strength and vigilance</u>.
8. <u>The griffin</u> <u>originated in the Middle East</u>.
9. <u>Pictures of it</u> <u>were found in the artwork of the ancient Babylonians and Assyrians</u>.
10. <u>The ancient Romans</u> <u>also created images of the griffin</u>.
11. <u>The griffin</u> <u>also appeared in medieval books</u>.
12. During the Middle Ages, <u>griffins</u> <u>sometimes served as gargoyles in Gothic architecture</u>.
13. <u>Maritza's best friend, Susannah,</u> <u>prefers to draw dragons</u>.
14. <u>The dragon</u> <u>symbolizes destruction, death, and evil in some belief systems</u>.
15. <u>Included in this group</u> are <u>the Mesopotamian, Hebrew, and Christian belief systems</u>.
16. In the English epic *Beowulf,* <u>the old hero</u> <u>slays a dragon but loses his own life</u>.

Answer Key **23**

LANGUAGE HANDBOOK 8 SENTENCES

17. Doesn't the legend of Saint George, the patron saint of England, describe his killing a dragon and rescuing a princess?
18. However, in some mythologies the dragon has beneficial powers.
19. According to the ancient Greeks and Romans, dragons could understand and reveal to humans the secrets of the earth.
20. Among the Celts, the dragon symbolized supreme political authority.
21. Later, the legendary creature appeared on the battle flags of English kings.
22. In Chinese mythology the dragon is a symbol of good fortune.
23. Parades in China on New Year's Day often feature a group of people wearing a long dragon costume.
24. This mock dragon is said to prevent misfortune in the new year.
25. In Chinese farming communities, some people credit dragons with controlling the rainfall and affecting the harvest.

WORKSHEET 4
Identifying the Simple Subject and the Simple Predicate
EXERCISE A
1. We | were eager to see the land so beautifully described by Pablo Neruda.
2. Our reservations on the flight | were quickly confirmed at the desk.
3. The flight attendant | welcomed all the passengers aboard the plane.
4. The engines | roared to life a few minutes later.
5. All the people on board | had by then fastened their seat belts.
6. The takeoff | was for me the most exciting part of the flight.
7. Captain Garcia | introduced herself over the intercom.
8. She | told us the altitude and speed of the airplane.
9. A dinner | was served on plastic trays.
10. Our flight to Chile | took ten hours.

EXERCISE B
1. Harriet Tubman—risked
2. people—marched
3. fox—streaked
4. lion—looks

5. Everyone—has signed
6. We—do copy
7. *You*—do forget
8. you—Have read
9. One—should help
10. dance—will be held

WORKSHEET 5
Identifying and Using Compound Subjects and Compound Verbs
EXERCISE A
1. Pandora—received, was
2. She—had been warned, opened
3. Despair, Disease—flew, frightened
4. Plague, Sorrow—followed
5. Hope—remained, gave
6. Io—suffered, was given
7. Zeus—loved, caused
8. She—was turned, was pursued
9. Peace, rest—came
10. she—was turned, had

EXERCISE B (Answers will vary.)
1. Marian, I
2. lifted, tied
3. Rashad, Harry
4. listened, sent
5. Knitting, crocheting
6. FDR, JFK
7. go, play
8. Melvin, Greg
9. been played, heard
10. *The Diary of a Young Girl, Woodsong*

WORKSHEET 6
Test
EXERCISE A
1. S—The summit of Mount Everest in the Himalayas is the highest point on earth.
2. F
3. S—Tenzing devoted his life to his dream of reaching the top of the great mountain.
4. F
5. S—Did Tenzing and Edmund P. Hillary make up one of the climbing teams?
6. F
7. F

24 Language Handbook Worksheets

LANGUAGE HANDBOOK 8 SENTENCES

8. F
9. S—Because his people have no written language, Tenzing could not write his own story.
10. S—James Ullman talked with Tenzing and wrote *Tiger of the Snows* for him.

EXERCISE B *(If students have not yet studied comma usage, do not grade for comma placement.)*

Today, there are still only thirteen stripes in the American flag, but there might have been fifty. ~~I~~ if Congress had not changed its mind. On January 1, 1776, General Washington flew the first flag of the United States. ~~T~~ the Grand Union flag. It had the flag of Great Britain in its corner and a stripe ~~F~~ for each of the original thirteen colonies. In 1777, Congress changed the flag. ~~B~~ by adding a blue field with thirteen stars. As new states entered the Union, ~~S~~ stars and stripes were added until, in 1818, Congress restored the original thirteen stripes.

EXERCISE C

1. Cesar Chavez | organized Californian farm workers in the 1960s.
2. One of his achievements | was a boycott of California grapes.
3. My friend Sharon | wants to be a meteorologist.
4. We | must soon consider the problem of global warming seriously.
5. Our high school courses | will affect our future jobs.
6. Some of my friends | will take vocational courses.
7. Other boys and girls | will prepare for college.
8. I | have not decided yet.
9. One of my cousins | has just started graduate school.
10. He | is studying the founding of the La Raza Unida Party in 1970.

EXERCISE D

1. The first Cajuns <u>moved to Louisiana from Canada</u>.
2. Today, the Cajun community in southwestern Louisiana <u>includes descendants of those immigrants</u>.
3. In the late 1800s, many Cajun landowners <u>were forced to sell their property</u>.
4. Many Cajuns <u>left Louisiana during the early part of the twentieth century</u>.
5. They <u>were attracted by the jobs in the new shipyards and refineries in eastern Texas</u>.
6. The Cajuns remaining in Louisiana <u>found their French language and culture under attack by the state government</u>.
7. Until the 1960s, all public school classes in Louisiana <u>had to be taught only in English</u>.
8. In the late 1960s, young Cajun college students <u>protested the suppression of their culture</u>.
9. Finally, the Louisiana state legislature <u>established the Council for the Development of French in Louisiana to help revive the Cajun culture</u>.
10. Today Cajun music and foods <u>are popular in many parts of the United States</u>.

EXERCISE E

1. farmers—are worrying
2. rain—has fallen
3. crops—Are wilting
4. cracks—have formed
5. sun—creeps
6. Clouds—have gathered
7. They—turn
8. farmers—are preparing
9. area—must rely
10. All—are hoping

EXERCISE F

1. Ezra Pound, Maya Angelou—are
2. committee—researched, wrote
3. Melissa, Beto—Does have
4. *You*—understand
5. One—seems
6. 1920s, 1960s—were
7. Rigoberta Menchú Tum—received, returned
8. you—would have chosen
9. frogs—are
10. musical—is based

LANGUAGE HANDBOOK 9 COMPLEMENTS

WORKSHEET 1
Identifying Subjects, Verbs, and Complements

EXERCISE *(The first item is the subject, the second is the verb, and the third is the complement.)*

1. John Glenn—has been—test pilot, astronaut, senator
2. He—has excelled
3. he—attended—Muskingum College
4. He—received—bachelor's degree
5. Glenn—joined—Marine Corps
6. he—flew—missions
7. He—piloted—fighters
8. Glenn—served
9. he—set—record
10. He—piloted—fighter
11. National Aeronautics and Space Administration—selected—Glenn, pilots
12. Glenn, astronauts—trained
13. NASA—gave—Glenn, opportunity
14. he—made—orbits
15. capsule—was called—*Friendship 7*
16. capsule—reached—altitude
17. Glenn—entered—politics
18. He—was elected
19. Glenn—was—senator
20. NASA—selected—Glenn

WORKSHEET 2
Identifying Direct Objects

EXERCISE A

1. teachings
2. squirrel
3. juice
4. piece
5. dinner
6. car
7. mitt
8. Aunt Edith
9. system
10. CDs

EXERCISE B *(The first item is the verb; the second is the direct object.)*

1. settled—NONE
2. formed—league
3. were—NONE
4. helped—NONE
5. created—some
6. honored—Hiawatha
7. used—name
8. joined—league
9. was—NONE
10. have—poems

WORKSHEET 3
Identifying Direct Objects and Indirect Objects

EXERCISE

1. video
2. granddaughter, stories
3. NONE
4. you, newspaper
5. NONE
6. us, card
7. award
8. NONE
9. Lawanda, Johnny, bread
10. friend, CD
11. cousin, note, photographs
12. songs
13. NONE
14. Venus
15. star
16. NONE
17. it, value
18. NONE
19. china
20. Rachel, ball
21. me, baseball, bat, collection
22. Booker Prize
23. coffee table
24. Jacob, me, advice
25. expectations

26 *Language Handbook Worksheets*

LANGUAGE HANDBOOK 9 COMPLEMENTS

WORKSHEET 4
Identifying Linking Verbs, Predicate Nominatives, and Predicate Adjectives

EXERCISE A
1. NONE
2. PN—teacher
3. NONE
4. PN—source
5. NONE
6. PA—together
7. PN—reporter
8. PA—beautiful
9. PA—strange
10. NONE

EXERCISE B
1. PA—is—active
2. PN—is—one
3. PN—became—lawyer
4. PA—seem—tame
5. PA—tastes—best
6. PA—looks—calm
7. PN—will be—member
8. PA—must remain—calm
9. PA—felt—hungry
10. PN—is—*A Tale of Two Cities*

WORKSHEET 5
Test

EXERCISE A *(The first item is the subject; the second item is the verb; the third is the complement(s).)*
1. sister—is—player
2. I—gave—her; mitt
3. She—was—happy
4. clerk—gave—Anna, Edwin; directions
5. running—improves—endurance, concentration
6. Stephanie—showed—us; picture
7. slope—looks—difficult
8. Professor Achebe—brought—class; souvenirs
9. *The Return of the King*—is—book
10. Tolkien—invented—languages

EXERCISE B
1. *The Red Badge of Courage*
2. teacher, note
3. NONE
4. you, bagel
5. children, swing set
6. NONE
7. Jerome, Sandy
8. me, sandwich, glass
9. books
10. Roberto, Tony, loan, advice

EXERCISE C
1. PA
2. DO
3. PA
4. PN
5. IO

EXERCISE D
1. PA—anxious
2. PN—body
3. DO—area
4. DO—bread
5. PA—famous
6. PN—source
7. PA—tricky
8. NONE
9. DO—salad
10. IO—girl; DO—prescription

Answer Key **27**

LANGUAGE HANDBOOK 10: KINDS OF SENTENCES

WORKSHEET 1
Identifying Simple and Compound Sentences

EXERCISE A
1. S
2. C—. . . groups, and . . .
3. C—. . . before, but . . .
4. S
5. S
6. S
7. S
8. S
9. C—. . . Blanding, or . . .
10. C

EXERCISE B *(Conjunctions may vary slightly.)*
1. . . . long, yet . . .
2. . . . later, for . . .
3. . . . instruments, but . . .
4. . . . hurry, or . . .
5. . . . roller coaster, so . . .

WORKSHEET 2
Identifying Independent and Subordinate Clauses

EXERCISE
1. The Populist movement was an American movement <u>that developed in the late 1800s.</u>
2. It began during the depression of the 1870s, <u>when farmers were losing money.</u>
3. The farmers organized cooperative groups, <u>which were called Farmers' Alliances.</u>
4. Members of these alliances hoped <u>that farmers' expenses could be reduced by selling supplies at lower prices.</u>
5. The alliances also built warehouses <u>so that farmers could store their crops until prices were better.</u>
6. Some alliances in the South included African American farmers.
7. <u>Even though African Americans were not allowed to vote,</u> the alliances included them.
8. <u>By 1891,</u> the movement was so strong <u>that it became a national political party.</u>
9. The alliances joined forces with an organization <u>that was called the Knights of Labor.</u>
10. The two groups formed the People's Party, <u>whose members were known as Populists.</u>
11. Populists wanted the national government to issue more paper money, <u>which might raise farm prices.</u>
12. The Populists wanted to form a national system <u>that was similar to the local co-ops.</u>
13. Populists also wanted a national income tax <u>so that taxes could be collected more fairly.</u>
14. <u>So that working people could have more leisure time,</u> the Populists wanted an eight-hour workday.
15. Populists pushed for the direct popular election of U.S. senators.
16. In 1892, the Populists had some success in the first national election <u>in which they took part.</u>
17. The Populists were strongest in 1896, <u>when William Jennings Bryan won the party's presidential nomination.</u>
18. <u>Even though Bryan was a Democrat,</u> he sympathized with the Populist cause.
19. <u>When the Populists endorsed Bryan,</u> they gave up their independent identity.
20. The brief Populist movement strongly influenced U.S. history, <u>because almost all of its principles were later made into law.</u>

WORKSHEET 3
Identifying Independent and Subordinate Clauses

EXERCISE
1. <u>I could not remember</u> where I put the serving dish, so <u>I went back to the kitchen to get another one.</u>
2. <u>Portraits of many family ancestors hung in the corridor</u> that ran the length of the house, yet <u>they were not clearly visible</u> because not enough light came through the window.
3. <u>Two hours was a long time to wait,</u> but <u>Rennie willingly sat in the musty parlor</u> while Samantha finished packing.
4. <u>On our vacation, we went to the Bay of Fundy,</u> which separates the Canadian provinces of New Brunswick and Nova Scotia, and <u>we witnessed one of the highest tides in the world.</u>
5. <u>In Greek mythology, the Hydra was a nine-headed monster</u> that lived in a marsh; when one of the heads was severed, <u>two grew in its place.</u>

28 *Language Handbook Worksheets*

LANGUAGE HANDBOOK 10 KINDS OF SENTENCES

6. Natalie wanted to have an autographed copy of Amy Tan's new book, so she purchased a copy and took it to the table in the bookstore where the author was sitting during a book-signing event.
7. Gabriela did not fully agree with the speaker, nor did she feel that he had focused enough on his topic.
8. When a television program is shot inside a studio, several cameras are often used; three or four cameras are focused on the same action at once, and the director chooses the best angle.
9. Chen wanted to take the Introduction to Computers course that was being taught on Monday and Wednesday mornings by Ms. Martelli, but his busy schedule prevented him from enrolling.
10. My family went to Costa Rica last summer, and my mother discovered that over a thousand species of orchids grow there.

WORKSHEET 4

Identifying Independent and Subordinate Clauses

EXERCISE

1. The student who scores highest on the exam will go to the finals, and the student with the second-highest score will receive special recognition at the annual awards banquet on May 25.
2. Don't believe everything that you read, for facts can be given a spin that makes them less reliable.
3. Yo-Yo Ma is an American cellist who is internationally known, and he has won ten Grammy Awards and several other awards for his recorded performances of both classical and popular music.
4. Before pottery was developed, food was eaten raw or roasted, but with pottery, people could cook in other ways.
5. Maribel explained that she had failed to take Tina's advice, for she had thought she knew better than Tina.
6. When my brother Tranh leaves for college at the Massachusetts Institute of Technology in Cambridge, I will move into his old bedroom, and I plan to paint it a more exciting color.
7. The South African runner Zola Budd attracted attention when she ran barefoot in competitions, yet running in her bare feet aggravated the injuries that she had already sustained.

8. The optician put drops in Rob's eyes, and when his pupils were dilated, she continued the exam.
9. You can wash the car and the sport utility vehicle now, but I would be happier if you would clean your room first.
10. Once Leah decided to run in the Over Hill and Dale Marathon, she began running six miles each weekday after school and band practice, and on weekends she averaged ten miles a day.

WORKSHEET 5

Classifying Sentences by Structure and by Purpose

EXERCISE A
1. S
2. CD-CX
3. S
4. CX
5. CD
6. CX
7. CX
8. CD
9. S
10. CX

EXERCISE B
1. INT ... ?
2. IMP ... .
3. DEC ... .
4. DEC ... .
5. DEC ... .
6. DEC ... .
7. INT ... ?
8. DEC ... .
9. EXC ... !
10. DEC ... .
11. INT ... ?
12. DEC ... .
13. DEC ... .
14. INT ... ?
15. IMP ... .
16. DEC ... .
17. INT ... ?
18. DEC ... .
19. DEC ... .
20. INT ... ?
21. EXC ... !
22. DEC ... .
23. IMP ... . (or !)
24. IMP ... .
25. DEC ... . (or EXC ... !)

Answer Key 29

LANGUAGE HANDBOOK 10 KINDS OF SENTENCES

WORKSHEET 6

Test

EXERCISE A
1. CD-CX
2. CD-CX
3. S
4. CD-CX
5. CD
6. CD-CX
7. CX
8. S
9. CD
10. CX

EXERCISE B
1. INT ... ?
2. DEC ... .
3. IMP ... .
4. INT ... ?
5. DEC ... .
6. EXC ... !
7. DEC ... .
8. DEC ... .
9. INT ... ?
10. EXC ... ! (or DEC ... .)

EXERCISE C
1. CX—IND
2. CD—IND
3. CX—SUB
4. CD-CX—SUB
5. CX—IND
6. CD—IND
7. CX—IND
8. CX—SUB
9. CX—IND
10. CX—SUB

EXERCISE D *(Sentences will vary.)*
1. Ronnie told me a story about his family that is hard to believe.
2. The books are on the top shelf of the bookcase that is in the hallway.
3. Rosetta will not go near the water, but she loves snow skiing.
4. Unless the train arrives on time, there is no hurry to get to the station.
5. Even though the dog is three months old, we have not started training her to walk on a leash, and I don't know when we'll get around to it.
6. Since Evan's grandfather had planted it, we thought the tree was very special, and we all gathered in front of it for a picture.
7. The Morrisons traveled throughout Central America, and they had some interesting adventures.
8. The song reminded Mary of something in her past, and she felt like a little girl again.
9. Please hurry with the photos so that Charlene can finish the project.
10. The moccasins were in an old chest, and we found them when we cleaned out the attic.

LANGUAGE HANDBOOK 11 WRITING EFFECTIVE SENTENCES

WORKSHEET 1
Correcting Run-on Sentences
EXERCISE

1. The St. Lawrence Seaway opened the Great Lakes to large ocean vessels. **A** cruise up the seaway makes a pleasant vacation.
2. Travelers may also take boat trips from Seattle to Victoria, British Columbia. **T**hen they can go on to Vancouver from Victoria.
3. C
4. Fine bone china cups and saucers are available. **C**ollecting these is a hobby for many people.
5. C
6. A trip through the Canadian Rockies is memorable. **M**any of the rugged mountains are covered with snow all summer.
7. C
8. The Calgary Stampede is a popular attraction. **I**t features bareback riding and other events.
9. The Canadian side of Niagara Falls is beautiful. **Y**ou can go right up to the Horseshoe Falls.
10. A trip to Ottawa, Ontario, should include a visit to the stately buildings of Canada's Parliament. **T**hey are built in the Gothic style.

WORKSHEET 2
Correcting and Revising Run-on Sentences
EXERCISE A

Today, when modern meteorologists forecast the weather, they can count on the help of an impressive battery of scientific devices. Weather satellites, for example, relay photographs of cloud formations from all over the world. **T**hese pictures show where storms are beginning over oceans and deserts. **T**he paths of typhoons and hurricanes are tracked in the same way. Weather information from all sources is fed into powerful computers. **T**hus the weather can be evaluated with amazing speed.

Our ancestors had no complicated weather instruments. **T**hey had to rely on their eyes and ears and a few old proverbs and maxims. Their methods were hardly scientific. **H**owever, some were founded on fact. Today, for example, no one still believes the old superstition about the groundhog, but we celebrate Groundhog Day just the same. If the groundhog sees its shadow on the second day of February, there will be six more weeks of winter. **W**atch for yourself and see! The behavior of insects, on the other hand, is still a good indicator of temperature because insects are cold-blooded. Grasshoppers cannot fly when the temperature drops below 55 degrees Fahrenheit. **I**f you hear a cricket chirping, count the number of chirps in fourteen seconds and add forty. **T**hen you will have the temperature in degrees Fahrenheit.

Today, weather forecasting is more accurate, if less picturesque, than it was in the old days. **H**owever, the forecasters are not always right, perhaps because there are so many factors to consider.

EXERCISE B *(Revisions may vary.)*

1. He invited me to visit him. **W**e went many places around Miami.
2. We could go to the animal park, **or** we could go to the aquarium, **but** we did not have time to go to both.
3. We went to the animal park, **and** I saw a Komodo dragon.
4. We also saw tree kangaroos. **T**hey are very cute.
5. C
6. The animals are not in cages, **but** they cannot get out.
7. The elephants live in big areas, **and** they are able to live normal lives.
8. Different exhibits deal with the continents of Asia, Africa, and Europe. **T**he Asian exhibit includes rare white Bengal tigers.
9. The African plains exhibit has giraffes, zebras, and ostriches living together as they do in the wild. **A** gorilla family also lives among them.
10. The animal park is the best one I ever visited. **I** hope to go back again soon.

WORKSHEET 3
Combining Choppy Sentences by Inserting Words
EXERCISE *(Revisions of sentence 5 may vary.)*

1. The Himalayas are the tallest mountains in Asia.
2. You can see a beautiful view of Mount Everest from Darjeeling.
3. Tea bushes grow on the steep, fertile slopes of the hills near Darjeeling.
4. The Sherpas are Tibetan people who live in northeast Nepal.

Answer Key **31**

LANGUAGE HANDBOOK 11 WRITING EFFECTIVE SENTENCES

5. Sherpa guide Tenzing Norgay was one of the first mountain climbers to reach the top of Mount Everest.
6. The greatest danger in mountain climbing comes from the high altitude and the bitter cold.
7. The bright sun reflecting on the white snow can cause temporary blindness.
8. The thin air at that high altitude makes expensive oxygen masks necessary.
9. The penetrating cold can cause severe frostbite on exposed fingers and toes.
10. Climbers need light, durable boots and nutritious food for reaching high altitudes.

WORKSHEET 4
Combining Choppy Sentences by Inserting Phrases

EXERCISE A *(Word order may vary in sentence 9.)*

1. Alexander the Great's father was the king of Macedonia.
2. When Alexander was young, he saw some wild horses in the marketplace.
3. One horse with a deep black coat threw anyone who dared to ride it.
4. Alexander's father, Philip, wanted to destroy the black horse with the mean temper.
5. Alexander noticed the shadow in front of the horse.
6. The horse's shadow moved on the ground as the horse jumped.
7. Alexander recognized the horse's fear of its own shadow.
8. He grabbed the reins on the horse and turned the animal around.
9. In this direction the horse no longer saw its frightening shadow on the ground.
10. The story about Alexander the Great taming the black horse is an example of his intelligence and compassion.

EXERCISE B *(Revisions may vary.)*

1. Employed by a large consulting firm, Nora is one of the firm's most successful consultants.
2. Carrying a mobile phone with her, she is able to answer her clients' questions at all times.
3. Known nationwide for her skill in solving computer problems, she is often the first person requested by a company in need.

4. Riding to the rescue, Nora is sometimes a company's last hope to save their computer files.
5. Regarded as one of the best by other members of her profession, last year she won an award from a national association of computer consultants.

WORKSHEET 5
Combining Choppy Sentences by Using *And*, *But*, or *Or*

EXERCISE A *(Revisions may vary slightly.)*

1. They will hike in Rocky Mountain National Park and pitch their tents in Hidden Valley.
2. Last year Marcy walked up Trail Ridge to the alpine meadows and went fishing in the Fall River.
3. Naomi and Marcy are interested in watching for bighorn sheep.
4. Sheep usually graze on the high slopes or wander down near Sheep Lake.
5. Marcy and Naomi have plenty of equipment for camping.
6. The pair will eat freeze-dried food or enjoy fish caught in the brooks and lakes.
7. Marcy or Naomi may clean the fish and cook them.
8. Naomi's father will drive out for the weekend and take them hiking above the timberline.
9. Camping and hiking are among the girls' favorite pastimes.
10. Both Marcy and Naomi are looking forward to the trip and are excited about camping in the mountains.

EXERCISE B *(Choice of conjunctions may vary.)*

1. Benjamin Franklin was an apprentice printer for his brother James, but he did not like working for him.
2. Franklin read many books after work, and in his writing he tried to copy the authors' styles.
3. Franklin and his brother printed the newspaper, and Franklin also had to sell the paper on the street.
4. U
5. Franklin could stay in Boston to work for his brother, or he could run away to seek his fortune.
6. He first went to New York City, but there was no work for printers in that city.

32 Language Handbook Worksheets

LANGUAGE HANDBOOK 11 WRITING EFFECTIVE SENTENCES

7. He took a ferry to Perth Amboy, New Jersey, and a storm drove the ferry onto the rocks.
8. U
9. Franklin finally started his own print shop, and it became successful very quickly.
10. Benjamin Franklin started *Poor Richard's Almanac*, and this publication made him famous.

WORKSHEET 6
Combining Choppy Sentences by Using Subordinate Clauses

EXERCISE A *(Revisions may vary slightly.)*

1. A newer park, which is four times the size of Yellowstone National Park, is called Gates of the Arctic National Park.
2. Many national parks are crowded with visitors, who may threaten the natural environment.
3. One national park in Hawaii contains active volcanoes that sometimes spew fire and lava.
4. Forest rangers, whom most people never see, work deep within the national forest.
5. At Mesa Verde National Park you can climb down into kivas that were built by ancient cliff dwellers.
6. My aunt Laura's job, which is filled with danger, is guiding rafts down the Colorado River.
7. In Virginia there is a national monument to Booker T. Washington, who made many contributions to education.
8. Dinosaur National Monument, which interests me the most of all monuments, is in Colorado.
9. Terry, who loves to camp by the sea, will enjoy Acadia National Park.
10. Rangers who live in tall watchtowers scan the horizon for forest fires.

EXERCISE B *(Order of clauses will vary.)*

1. Many people want to be ballet dancers because ballet dancing seems to be a glamorous profession.
2. The United States Constitution will last another two hundred years if we maintain our love for freedom.
3. When we were seven or eight years old, we sat through movie matinees every Saturday.
4. Since she won the election last year, Melinda is not eligible to run again.
5. Preston wants to exercise every day so that he can stay fit.

6. Wherever there are hungry bears and unguarded campsites, there is trouble.
7. Although the choice of merchandise is limited, we will do all our shopping in this store.
8. Unless he or she begins training very early, an athlete has no chance to enter the Olympics.
9. While the batter took some practice swings, the pitcher threw warm-up tosses.
10. Marsha had already received her prize in the mail before Phil collected all thirty-three box tops.

WORKSHEET 7
Revising Stringy and Wordy Sentences

EXERCISE A *(Revisions will vary.)*

1. Tanmoor is an interesting character in a story Jessica wrote. He is from a small town in Argentina, but he wants to go to a big city.
2. The story about Tanmoor has an exciting beginning. It opens with his father working on a ranch.
3. Some rustlers come to the ranch, and a group of bankers arrives. Some angry neighbors visit, and tension mounts.
4. Tanmoor's father is a *vaquero*, a cowboy. *Vaqueros* have a lot of responsibility.
5. Tanmoor's father, named Carlos but nicknamed Coco, is trusted by the ranch owners.
6. Tanmoor helps his father and enjoys the work, but he wants to own his own business in the city.
7. A smart boy, he likes to figure out people, so he watches their expressions and movements.
8. Tanmoor identifies the rustlers and tricks the bankers. Then he calms the neighbors, restoring peace to the ranch.
9. Jessica modeled the character Tanmoor after her brother, Tom Andrew Moore.
10. Tom Moore reads a lot about South America and can tell you all about its major cities.

EXERCISE B *(Revisions will vary.)*

1. I usually order a large salad when we eat out.
2. After the game ended, my voice was hoarse from yelling.
3. With a quick movement of her fingers, Nana turned the hot tortillas.
4. Mariah knows all of the state capitals.
5. We passed the pavilion as a woman yelled loudly.

Answer Key 33

LANGUAGE HANDBOOK 11 WRITING EFFECTIVE SENTENCES

6. Have you memorized the "I Have a Dream" speech by Martin Luther King, Jr.?
7. Much to the astonishment of everyone there, the window did not break.
8. The scientist closely examined the insect.
9. Before the class resumes, we can go over our homework.
10. The thunder was alarmingly loud.

WORKSHEET 8
Test

EXERCISE A *(Revisions will vary.)*
1. Believers in the movement are frozen upon death, and their bodies are kept in special temperature-controlled units.
2. Scientists may eventually find cures for all terminal diseases. Patients in cryonic suspension will then be brought back to life.
3. Science fiction writers often include suspended animation in their stories and films. They use it to explain how astronauts could make journeys lasting hundreds of years.
4. In the movie *Planet of the Apes,* astronauts put themselves into suspended animation for a long space voyage, and when they wake up, they find themselves on a planet inhabited by intelligent apes.
5. Several sequels to this movie have been produced. One sequel features the apes releasing an alien virus.

EXERCISE B *(Revisions will vary.)*

Hurricanes are powerful tropical storms that form over warm ocean water near the equator. In a second, a hurricane can produce as much energy as several thousand atomic bombs, spread over an area of several hundred miles. Winds in a hurricane blow more than 75 miles per hour and sometimes reach 120 miles per hour. Hurricanes move over land, causing great devastation with their winds. Now meteorologists track hurricanes accurately and predict their paths so that people can be evacuated before a hurricane arrives.

Emily Dickinson, who lived during the nineteenth century, has become an interesting subject for biographers. She wrote a great deal of poetry, chiefly for herself but sometimes for a few friends. She wrote many of her beautiful poems on scraps of paper that she hid in a drawer. For a short while, she studied at Mount Holyoke Female Seminary in Massachusetts, and then she became a recluse. She seldom left her house and always wore white dresses. No one knows exactly why.

EXERCISE C *(Revisions will vary.)*
1. The puppy ran into the street while it was raining. The car skidded, but it missed the puppy.
2. Although the assignment was long and I was tired, it was so easy that I finished before supper.
3. The movie started on time, but we were late and missed the first ten minutes. I was upset.
4. I am allowed to miss school tomorrow for Rosh Hashana, which is the Jewish New Year.
5. Oxford shoes are popular now. My brother has a black pair that I like.

EXERCISE D *(Revisions will vary.)*
1. I proudly accepted the award.
2. After the dance we went for a walk along the beach.
3. You will always be welcome in my home.
4. Make sure you sharpen all your pencils before you take the test.
5. The mamba is a tree snake that comes from Africa.

34 Language Handbook Worksheets

LANGUAGE HANDBOOK 12 CAPITAL LETTERS

WORKSHEET 1
Using Capital Letters Correctly
EXERCISE A
1. *D*id Ms. Lamas say, "*F*ill the piñatas for Cinco de Mayo"?
2. My sister is so dramatic; every morning she says, "*G*reetings, *O* dawn of a new day!"
3. Joyce Kilmer wrote a poem that begins, "I think that *I* shall never see / A poem lovely as a tree."
4. *T*he results of the spelling bee prove that *I* can think under pressure.
5. The minister ended her prayer by saying, "*H*ear us, *O* Lord, today and always."
6. The most recent story we read for class was "The Treasure of Lemon Brown" by *W*alter *D*ean *M*yers.
7. After reading the story, we discussed Lemon Brown's statement, "*E*very man got a treasure."
8. Should Jamie and *I* go to the library now or later?
9. *O*ur town's sister city is *S*aumur, *F*rance.
10. The voice over the loudspeaker said, "*F*lash floods are expected. *S*chool will be dismissed at noon."

EXERCISE B
Last summer my family and *I* went to Mandan, *N*orth *D*akota, to see the dedication of a monument to American Indian cultures. We attended a nighttime ceremony, where a speaker began by saying, "*W*e are one with you and each other, *O* Great Spirit." As we sat on the ground under the constellation *O*rion and thousands of other stars, I felt a strong connection with the universe. The next day we visited Fort Abraham Lincoln State *P*ark where the Heart *R*iver and the *M*issouri *R*iver meet.

WORKSHEET 2
Capitalizing Proper Nouns
EXERCISE
1. B
2. A
3. B
4. B
5. A
6. A
7. B
8. B
9. A
10. A
11. B
12. A
13. B
14. B
15. A
16. B
17. B
18. A
19. A
20. B
21. B
22. A
23. B
24. A
25. B

WORKSHEET 3
Capitalizing Proper Nouns
EXERCISE A
1. Although she now lives in the *E*ast, she liked living in *C*alifornia best.
2. Her family lived in *C*hicago, *N*ew *Y*ork, *S*t. *L*ouis, and *S*an *F*rancisco.
3. The *U*nderwoods have tried to learn about each area where they have lived.
4. C
5. Now they live in a suburb north of *B*oston called *W*ayland and swim in *L*ake *C*ochichuate.
6. When the *U*nderwoods lived in *S*an *F*rancisco, their house was only a block from *S*an *F*rancisco *B*ay.
7. Betty loved to cross the *G*olden *G*ate *B*ridge and ride the cable cars on *C*alifornia *S*treet.
8. Her sister, *A*licia, attended classes at the *U*niversity of *C*alifornia at *B*erkeley.
9. There she studied world religions like *B*uddhism and *I*slam.
10. Followers of *I*slam are called *M*uslims.
11. When the family moved to *S*t. Louis, they had trouble finding a home near the water.
12. The *M*ississippi *R*iver is too muddy to swim in, and its current is very swift.
13. In *C*hicago, the family lived in *W*ilmette at 187 *T*enth *A*venue.
14. They often saw the *C*hicago *C*ubs play at *W*rigley *F*ield.
15. The baseball field is at 1060 *W*est *A*ddison *B*oulevard.
16. After she graduates from high school, Betty would like to attend the *U*niversity of *C*hicago, which is in *H*yde *P*ark.
17. She wants to study the art of ancient *G*reece.
18. C
19. She wants to live in *P*aris and study at the *U*niversity of *P*aris.
20. Betty would visit the *L*ouvre and study the paintings of *M*onet and *C*assatt.

EXERCISE B
1. Have you ever been to southern *C*alifornia?
2. Isn't *G*ary, *I*ndiana, near *C*hicago?
3. Daniel was awarded a *P*urple *H*eart for bravery in the *V*ietnam *W*ar.
4. My mother recently read a biography of the anthropologist *M*argaret *M*ead.

Answer Key 35

LANGUAGE HANDBOOK 12 CAPITAL LETTERS

5. Hudson **B**ay is very far north, beyond **L**ake **S**uperior.
6. My mother met my father on the ferry to **C**ape **C**harles, **V**irginia.
7. The north wind is quite cold in **C**algary, **A**lberta.
8. Most of the religions in the world are based on belief in **G**od, the supreme being. (*or* **S**upreme **B**eing)
9. Let's go swimming in **C**hippewa **L**ake.
10. Charles **L**indbergh was the first person to fly solo across the **A**tlantic **O**cean.
11. I will start my job with the **C**.**O**. **M**iller **C**ompany next **M**onday.
12. We are studying the art of the **I**talian **R**enaissance.
13. Classes at **W**ade **J**unior **H**igh **S**chool start on the **T**hursday after **L**abor **D**ay.
14. The National **S**cience **F**air takes place right after spring vacation.
15. I enjoyed the **M**ichigan **S**tate **F**air, which opened last **S**aturday.
16. Veterans **D**ay was originally called **A**rmistice **D**ay, in commemoration of the end of **W**orld **W**ar I on **N**ovember 11, 1918.
17. We visited the **U**nited **S**tates **S**enate, the **H**ouse of **R**epresentatives, and the **T**reasury **B**uilding during our student tour of **W**ashington, D.C.
18. They attended **M**artin **L**uther **K**ing, **J**r., **H**igh **S**chool in **A**kron, **O**hio.
19. The **M**oon **L**amp **C**ompany has a mailing address at **G**rand **C**entral **S**tation.
20. During the fall and winter there are several holidays, such as **T**hanksgiving, **C**hristmas, and New **Y**ear's **D**ay.
21. Patrick and **C**olleen **M**urphy make a wonderful **I**rish stew of mutton and vegetables.
22. Our neighbor **J**ames **D**owden plans to take a long vacation to **A**ustralia, **N**ew **Z**ealand, and **H**ong **K**ong.
23. In 1998 and 1999, NASA launched six separate spacecraft in six months, including **D**eep **S**pace 1 and **M**ars **P**olar **L**ander.
24. This summer my family and the **J**ohnson family are driving to the **P**etrified **F**orest **N**ational **P**ark in **A**rizona.
25. Mount **W**hitney is the highest peak in the **S**ierra **N**evada in eastern **C**alifornia.

WORKSHEET 4

Capitalizing Proper Adjectives and School Subjects

EXERCISE A

1. Most jazz rhythms come from **A**frican music.
2. Great jazz can be heard in many **L**ouisiana cities.
3. The original jazz bands were the **B**ourbon **S**treet groups, which marched in funerals in New Orleans.
4. Two famous **A**frican **A**merican jazz performers were Billie Holiday and Duke Ellington.
5. West **I**ndian music, such as the **C**aribbean calypso, is a mixture of **A**frican and **S**panish influences.
6. The **J**amaican steel bands produce a unique sound.
7. Some **J**amaican musicians play fantastic music on instruments made from old oil drums and other scrap materials.
8. In Puerto Rico, one needs to know the **S**panish language to enjoy oneself fully.
9. Puerto Ricans have always been very proud of their **L**atin **A**merican heritage.
10. Most tourists come back from Puerto Rico eager to learn **C**aribbean dances.

EXERCISE B

1. That row of houses is an excellent example of **G**eorgian architecture.
2. Will astronomy be covered in **S**cience I?
3. My father collects **D**anish glassware.
4. We had some **F**rench toast for breakfast.
5. The radio announcer spoke with an **E**nglish accent.
6. You can still see **M**oorish designs in some cities in Spain.
7. The modern helicopter was first flown by a **R**ussian **A**merican scientist.
8. This is not a typical **N**ew **E**ngland village.
9. Because it was a special dinner, we served **I**ndian food.
10. I'm very interested in **M**iddle **E**astern history.

36 Language Handbook Worksheets

LANGUAGE HANDBOOK 12 CAPITAL LETTERS

WORKSHEET 5
Capitalizing Proper Adjectives and School Subjects

EXERCISE
1. C
2. That restaurant specializes in *I*talian cooking.
3. Nester signed up for second-year *G*erman.
4. C
5. Were you there when Aunt Fiona taught us how to dance a *S*cottish fling?
6. The bossa nova is a type of *S*outh *A*merican music.
7. The art museum recently purchased some ancient *M*aya sculptures.
8. Professor Jansen is preparing her notes for a course in *R*oman history.
9. In college, Alfred will be majoring in *E*nglish.
10. C
11. The field trip to New Mexico will focus on *N*avajo culture.
12. My brother plans to take *L*atin I during his first semester and *S*panish I his second semester.
13. I bought my father a book about *M*editerranean food for his birthday.
14. Mumtaz and her family are going on an *A*laskan cruise next summer.
15. Joel and Eva plan to attend a *C*ajun festival this weekend in Louisiana.
16. This week our *E*nglish class will be studying a form of *J*apanese poetry known as haiku.
17. Do you enjoy hearing about the heroic deeds in *G*reek and *R*oman myths?
18. Yes, I do, and I also enjoy uncovering the moral lessons illustrated by many *A*frican *A*merican folk tales.
19. Numerous *A*merican *I*ndian myths describe ways that elements of the universe were created.
20. C

WORKSHEET 6
Capitalizing Titles

EXERCISE A
1. We read *T*he *D*iary of *A*nne *F*rank and then saw the play.
2. The *S*ecretary of *D*efense under *P*resident Lyndon Johnson was Robert McNamara.
3. My little brother's favorite TV program is *The Magic School Bus.*
4. I really like the comic strip "*P*eanuts," don't you?
5. Have you read the story "*T*he *C*ircuit" by Francisco Jiménez?
6. Abraham Lincoln worked closely with *S*ecretary of *S*tate William Seward.
7. After Liz saw the movie *T*itanic, she kept singing the song, "*M*y *H*eart *W*ill *G*o *O*n."
8. Please tell *C*aptain Jackson that I will be ten minutes late.
9. Tomás spent the summer in Mexico with *A*unt Rosa.
10. Greta loved Paul Theroux's book about train travel, *T*he *O*ld *P*atagonian *E*xpress.

EXERCISE B
1. In the Greek play *O*edipus *R*ex the gods play a major role in people's lives.
2. Aunt Edna, have you seen our copy of the Sunday edition of *T*he *N*ews and *O*bserver?
3. The book I am reading, *B*aseball *I*s a *F*unny *G*ame, is very amusing.
4. At the meeting, *P*resident Polanski proposed that we sponsor a local soccer team.
5. My sister shook hands with the *S*ecretary of *S*tate last week.
6. We are going to watch *U*ncle Leo repair the calliope from the Barnum & Bailey Circus.
7. One of Texas's most respected representatives was *C*ongresswoman Barbara Jordan.
8. Ms. Jenkins wants us to memorize "*C*asey at the *B*at" for assembly.
9. When Jamaica became independent, the United States was represented at the ceremonies by *V*ice *P*resident Johnson.
10. If you are interested in horses, I would certainly recommend *K*ing of the *W*ind by Marguerite Henry.

LANGUAGE HANDBOOK 12 CAPITAL LETTERS

WORKSHEET 7
Test

EXERCISE A
1. The African country Morocco would be fun to visit.
2. We studied it in history class last year, and I learned that most Moroccans are Muslim.
3. From 1912 to 1956, part of Morocco was divided into French and Spanish zones and was ruled by those countries.
4. The kingdom is now united, with the city of Rabat as its capital.
5. Would you rather have lived during the Stone Age, the Bronze Age, or the Iron Age?
6. Cory asked, "Should I take Algebra II or geometry next year?"
7. Gunnar's parents donated new Macintosh® computers for the graphics classes.
8. Felicia loves math and takes Calculus 201 at the junior college on Saturdays.
9. The English class is more challenging than the science class this semester.
10. Next year my electives will be Art I, Latin, and tennis.
11. When the bell rang, I ran to my Geography II class.
12. We have an Irish setter named Fergus.
13. "The Inn of Lost Time" by Lensey Namioka has a story within the story.
14. Carmen asked, "Is Labor Day always on a Monday?"
15. Do you know the song "American Pie"?
16. Where did Ms. Novich put the recipe for tomatillo salsa?
17. They took the train City of New Orleans to Chicago to hear Jesse Jackson speak.
18. Jon's uncle was awarded a Nobel Prize in economics last year.
19. We recited the poem "O Captain! My Captain!" at the Fourth of July celebration.
20. We saw Venus bright in the sky as we drove to the Texas Rangers game.
21. This weekend, we will attend the Colorado State Fair in Pueblo.
22. Did you rent a video of the animated film Antz?
23. Noah plans to see the Washington Monument during his spring break.
24. "The chair recognizes Senator Smith," announced Chairman Jones.
25. Heidi and Bob rented skis at the resort in Squaw Valley, California.

EXERCISE B
1. Thomas Jefferson was the president (or President) who negotiated the Louisiana Purchase.
2. One of my favorite books is Robert Louis Stevenson's Treasure Island.
3. C
4. Yesterday in class we read the poem "The Toaster."
5. Sometimes the wind that blows off Lake Michigan is very cold.
6. Have you read the story "The Landlady" yet?
7. My cousin is an aide to Ambassador Mabel Smythe.
8. The city of Jerusalem is sacred to Muslims, Christians, and Jews.
9. In 1994, Nelson Mandela was elected president (or President) of South Africa.
10. One of the magazines at the dentist's office is Highlights for Children.
11. Will you be entering your strawberry preserves in this year's Strawberry Festival?
12. C
13. I read in the newspaper that a Grecian vase was stolen from the museum.
14. Mr. Carlyle loves to read about English history.
15. On Saturday the Garcia family took a hike along Barton Creek.
16. C
17. Your appointment with Professor Wilson is on Wednesday, August 15.
18. C
19. Will we be taking History II next semester?
20. My aunt Luisa is a member of the Ohio State Historical Society.
21. The Battle of San Juan Hill was fought during the Spanish-American War.
22. Did you see Congresswoman Waters at the press conference?
23. This year we'll be spending Thanksgiving with our grandfather.
24. C
25. Today I would like to announce my candidacy for the United States Senate.

38 Language Handbook Worksheets

LANGUAGE HANDBOOK 12 CAPITAL LETTERS

EXERCISE C

Anyone who has studied **U**nited **S**tates history knows that our country was settled by people from many lands. Not all of us, however, realize how much the customs of these other lands still influence our daily life.

A glance at a map of the **U**nited States shows some of the main foreign influences in each region's names. In the **E**ast we find many **D**utch names like **R**ensselaer, **B**rooklyn, and **S**chenectady. In the **W**est and **S**outhwest we find **S**panish names like San **F**rancisco and Nevada. In the **M**idwest and the **S**outh, **F**rench explorers and settlers left their mark in names like La Crosse and Dubuque, Baton **R**ouge and **N**ew Orleans.

New Orleans, indeed, is a good example of the way other cultures have affected **A**merican life. Many of its streets still bear such French names as Toulouse **S**treet and **G**ravier Street. Restaurants there are famous for their **F**rench dishes. The architecture of the French **Q**uarter, however, looks more **S**panish than **F**rench, reflecting many years of **S**panish rule.

The influences that have shaped our country turn up in some surprising places. Many of **W**ashington, **D.C.**'s monuments, for example, have the classic lines of a **G**reek temple dedicated to the ancient gods. In the **S**outheast, a few mansions built before the American **C**ivil **W**ar recall the same architecture. Some of **C**alifornia's churches, founded by early **C**atholic missionaries, would be equally at home in Mexico.

America's food, too, has been influenced by many cultures. Who has not at some time enjoyed **C**hinese egg drop soup, **I**talian pasta, **M**exican tacos, or the **G**erman and **S**candinavian cheeses of **W**isconsin? The smorgasbord may seem **A**merican, but the idea originated in **S**weden. Pretzels were originally **D**utch delicacies. Shish kebab, which is often served at backyard barbecues, is actually a **T**urkish dish. Bagels and knishes are popular **J**ewish dishes. No **T**hanksgiving dinner would be complete without turkey, corn, and pumpkin. These foods are truly **A**merican, for they came to us from the **A**merican Indians who lived here long before the **P**ilgrims reached **N**orth America.

Answer Key **39**

LANGUAGE HANDBOOK 13 PUNCTUATION

WORKSHEET 1
Using End Marks

EXERCISE A
1. ... Missouri.
2. ... house?
3. ... records.
4. ... be!
5. ... fascinating. (or ... fascinating!)
6. ... job?
7. ... hobby.
8. ... hobby?
9. ... out.
10. ... past.

EXERCISE B *(Wording may vary slightly.)*
1. Is someone going to repair this typewriter?
2. You said the beach is two miles from here.
3. Will you write the report tomorrow?
4. You were waiting to see me, young man.
5. Does the line reach the end of the block?

WORKSHEET 2
Using End Marks and Periods After Abbreviations

EXERCISE A
1. ... ground.
2. ... anthills?
3. ... road!
4. ... driveway.
5. ... of it.
6. ... protection?
7. ... Spanish.
8. ... Oklahoma.
9. ... Saturday.
10. ... it! (or ... it.)

EXERCISE B
1. Your appointment this Thursday at 2 P.M. is with Dr. Vergese.
2. Have you ever read any books by J. D. Salinger or W. H. Auden?
3. The famous standing stones at Stonehenge date from 2000 B.C., which is about 1100 years after the first structures at the site.
4. Please send the package to Ms. B. D. Chan, P. O. Box 1138, Ann Arbor, MI 48104.

5. Which sounds better, Martin Luther King, Jr., Blvd. or Martin Luther King, Jr., Ave.?
6. My brother J. J. has pinned to his bulletin board a picture of St. Augustine, Fla., which was founded in A.D. 1565.
7. The author P. J. O'Rourke was interviewed on CNN about his opinion on the change in leadership at the UN.
8. My mother received her M.D. from Columbia University in New York, N.Y., and she did her residency at Brackenridge Hospital in Austin, Tex.
9. Isn't Mrs. Jergens a member of the Parents and Teachers Assn.?
10. The length of the curtains has been trimmed from 1 yd to 34 in. so that the hem won't drag on the windowsill.

WORKSHEET 3
Using Commas to Separate Words and Phrases and After Introductory Elements

EXERCISE A *(If you permit students to omit the final series comma, then the commas that are underscored below may be considered optional.)*
1. Mrs. Jones stopped her car, opened the door, and walked to a telephone booth near the roadside.
2. For lunch we had soup, salad, and banana bread.
3. Where we will go, when we will leave, and how long we will stay are problems yet to be settled.
4. Dr. Solomon ordered bandages, liniment, and rest for my foot.
5. I soaked my foot, rubbed it, and walked very little for several days.
6. Orange juice, cereal, and vegetables are on the grocery list.
7. After a hot, muggy afternoon, we had a violent thunderstorm. *(The comma after* afternoon *is optional.)*
8. As long as you plan to go downtown, will you pick up a train schedule at the station for me?
9. In its annual report to the public, the Salt Lake City weather bureau announced that we had experienced the coldest winter since 1897.
10. The hound chased the rabbit across the meadow, through the swamp, and into the woods.

40 Language Handbook Worksheets

LANGUAGE HANDBOOK 13 PUNCTUATION

11. The long, dark pathway led to a grim, ruined house.
12. The movie was advertised as gigantic, stupendous, and colossal.
13. All seventh-grade, eighth-grade, and ninth-grade boys should report to the gym.
14. The enormous, white, drifting snowflakes were beautiful.
15. Skating, hockey, and skiing classes will begin in January.
16. After a month of beautiful weather, the past three Saturdays have been windy, cold, and rainy.
17. We saw the biologists come back with a long, scary rattlesnake.
18. Coretta found a red, hand-knit ski hat for her boyfriend.
19. Our lunchroom is bright, cheerful, noisy, and efficient.
20. Now that winter's coming, I am looking for a pair of warm, black gloves.

WORKSHEET 4
Using Commas in Compound Sentences and with Interrupters

EXERCISE A

1. I did not have a book about her at home, so I found one at the public library.
2. I read it some time ago, yet the story stays fresh in my mind.
3. She was given the name Isabella as a child, but she gave up the name eventually.
4. She chose the name Sojourner Truth, for it reflected her religious beliefs.
5. Some sources say she was born in 1797, but no one knows for certain.
6. She learned about the movement to abolish slavery, and she became one of the movement's most effective speakers.
7. Some might remember her best as an abolitionist, or they might remember her as a women's rights advocate.
8. The stories of slaves' lives are very sad, yet we should read and learn from them.
9. The struggle against slavery was hard, yet Sojourner Truth never gave up.
10. She did not stop fighting for the rights of freed slaves after slavery was abolished, nor did she lessen her support for women's causes.

EXERCISE B

1. The tamales, just out of the pot and steaming on a platter, looked too good to resist.
2. The stray cat, by the way, has made herself at home on our porch.
3. The championship game, postponed by rain, resumed last night.
4. The millpond, glittering in the moonlight, looked lovely.
5. If I clean my room, Mother, may I go to the party?
6. My uncle Cecil, who was a navigator in the Air Force, taught me the constellations.
7. Toni Cade Bambara, one of my favorite writers, once spoke at the local college.
8. Sasha, don't forget to return those books to the library.
9. Our oldest dog, Wilbur, loves to ride in the car.
10. Amy Tan, who wrote *The Joy Luck Club*, was born in Oakland, California.

WORKSHEET 5
Using Commas with Interrupters and with Introductory Words, Phrases, and Clauses

EXERCISE A

1. Our newest neighbor, Dr. Stearns, is a veterinarian.
2. She has a marvelous gift with animals, I'm sure.
3. For example, even a gentle dog will bite when it is hurt.
4. The sickest dog seems to know, however, that Dr. Stearns is its friend.
5. Not long ago a stray dog was hit by a delivery truck on Carter Drive, a street near the doctor's house.
6. Well, Dr. Stearns ran out of the house when she heard the noise.
7. "Can you do anything, Doc?" someone asked.
8. The dog, a big yellow mongrel, let her come near without a growl.
9. She took care of the dog for quite a while, three months altogether.
10. The dog, thank goodness, experienced a full recovery.

Answer Key 41

LANGUAGE HANDBOOK 13 PUNCTUATION

EXERCISE B

1. No, I have never tried herbal tea.
2. By the time Keith and Carl had driven through the rain to Tulsa, they decided not to go any farther.
3. From the depths of his vivid imagination, Ray Bradbury creates fascinating stories.
4. Born and raised in a Mexican American neighborhood in Fresno, Gary Soto draws on his own life for his writing.
5. After she read *The Haunting of Hill House*, Millie refused to answer the door after dark.
6. As the highest peak in New England, New Hampshire's Mount Washington stands 6,288 feet tall.
7. To view the three spectacular waterfalls, people traveling through the Columbia River Gorge in Oregon must take the old road.
8. Well, why don't you give her a call?
9. Stunned by the assassination of Martin Luther King, Jr., in 1968, many people wept.
10. Standing together after winning the championship, the team happily received the cheers and applause.

WORKSHEET 6
Using Commas for Dates and Addresses and in Letters

EXERCISE A

1. My sister was born on Monday, February 7, 1983, at 3 P.M.
2. Our town was shut down from February 1 to February 5, 1993, by a blizzard.
3. The publishing company is located at 757 Third Avenue, New York, New York 10017.
4. The building stands on the corner of Fifth Avenue and Fiftieth Street, New York City.
5. The school play will be repeated on Friday, April 3, and Saturday, April 4.
6. C
7. Our pastor comes from a town near Pittsburgh, Pennsylvania.
8. The finals will be played at Evanston Township High School, Evanston, Illinois.
9. Please send the book to 2107 Carney Avenue, Baltimore, MD 21234.
10. The project will run until November 17, 2002.
11. The doctor will see you next Tuesday, June 23.
12. The cookbook came from 1776 Ashland Circle, Boise, ID 83705.
13. The deadline fell on the afternoon of Friday, August 31.
14. C
15. The fictional detective Sherlock Holmes lived at 221B Baker Street, London, England.
16. C
17. The famous singer's birthplace still stands at 85 Sheridan Avenue, Hohokus, NJ 07423.
18. C
19. The sporting goods shop is located at Green Acres Shopping Center, Sunrise Highway, Valley Stream, New York.
20. Soon after 5 o'clock on Tuesday, June 24, 1980, we saw the meteor hit the ground.

EXERCISE B

[1] My great-great-grandfather on my father's side was born in Calhoun County, South Carolina, on March 2, 1898. [2] He grew up in a house at 1716 Cedar Street, Weldon, North Carolina, in the northern part of the state. [3] My great-great-grandmother was born in Charleston, South Carolina, on August 23, 1902. [4] As a girl, she grew up just around the corner from her future husband, at 210 East Sixth Street. [5] She was several years younger than he, however, and he never paid much attention to her until September 12, 1917, just before he went off to war with the Weldon volunteers. [6] He was stationed in Paris, France. [7] He came back on leave to marry his sweetheart, in New York, New York. [8] They were married on Saturday, December 28, 1918. [9] They moved to Texas soon after my great-great-grandfather got out of the army in 1919. [10] On December 15, 1928, they moved from Dime Box to the city, where they lived in the same house for the rest of their lives, at 3 Park Terrace, Houston, Texas.

EXERCISE C

March 11, 2000

Dear Josie,

Here's my new address: 1352 Sycamore Street, Fillmore, TX 73214. We've been so busy! After moving into the new house, we spent several days arranging and rearranging things. Yes, we did get a dog from the animal shelter now that we have a fenced yard. Before we had a chance to decide on a name, my little brother started calling him Bubba.

LANGUAGE HANDBOOK 13 PUNCTUATION

Remember not to use our old address—343 Ardmore Avenue, Houston, Texas—when you write.

Your friend,

Anna

WORKSHEET 7

Using Semicolons and Colons

EXERCISE A

1. There are five kinds of prairie dogs; the black-tailed is the most numerous.
2. Black-tailed prairie dogs live in the plains of Mexico, Texas, New Mexico, Oklahoma, and other states; white-tailed prairie dogs live in areas of Arizona, New Mexico, Utah, Colorado, and Wyoming.
3. In prairie dog country you can often see prairie dog towns; every mound of dirt indicates the entrance to a prairie dog tunnel.
4. The mounds are used as lookout points; that is, the prairie dogs stand on the mounds to watch for predators.
5. If a prairie dog spots a predator, it gives a high-pitched bark that warns all the prairie dogs to go underground; as a result, most prairie dogs escape the danger.
6. The mounds also serve as water barriers; otherwise, the burrows would flood during heavy rains.
7. In open country prairie dog tunnels may stretch for miles; the tunnels can house hundreds of family groups called coteries.
8. Along the tunnels, each coterie has its own underground rooms; and each room has a particular purpose, such as for sleeping, nursing babies, or storing food.
9. Baby prairie dogs stay with their parents for one year; the following spring, the young leave to start families of their own.
10. Prairie dogs do not hibernate; instead, they spend the winters underground living off the seeds and grasses they have stored.

EXERCISE B

1. The class begins promptly at 8:30 tomorrow morning.
2. I only want to know one thing: Where did you put the casserole dish?
3. Read these poems for class tomorrow: "Paul Revere's Ride" and "Barbara Frietchie."
4. Both poems are in the section titled "The American Hero: Myth and Reality."
5. The verse from the Bible that I want you to consider is Second Corinthians 3:6.

WORKSHEET 8

Test

EXERCISE A (If you permit students to omit the final series comma, then the commas that are underscored below may be considered optional.)

1. Wow! Look at the size of that tiger!
2. To make the posters, of course, we need markers, water colors, and stencils.
3. Do you know, Mandy, that Jack London lived to be only forty years old?
4. Above the rooftop of the apartment building, we saw a beautiful, bright rainbow.
5. Phillip, unplug the table saw right now. (or !)
6. Casey and I are going to make enchiladas for the fiesta; Lillian is making salsa. (or ... fiesta, Lillian ...)
7. For the chalupas Patrick will make baked, crisp corn tortillas.
8. Let's each bring a real plate, a cloth napkin, and tableware so that we don't use throwaway items.
9. Our fiesta will be held on September 16, 2000; that is the anniversary of the beginning of the 1810 Mexican rebellion against Spain.
10. We will have food, games, and piñatas; and a folk group will sing, play, and dance.

EXERCISE B (If you permit students to omit the final series comma, then the commas that are underscored below may be considered optional.)

1. Wanting to play drums very well, Logan practiced every day.
2. Their mailing address has been changed to P.O. Box 312, Carrizozo, New Mexico.
3. Do you enjoy computer-animated films like *Toy Story*?
4. What a brilliant meteor that is!
5. Planting the seeds, watering them, and weeding the area usually results in healthy growth.
6. Kwanzaa, an African American holiday, is celebrated between Dec. 26 and Jan. 1.
7. Sonia, please get off the phone.
8. The tall, graceful sycamore tree by our house is dying; it will have to be cut down soon.

Answer Key 43

LANGUAGE HANDBOOK 13 PUNCTUATION

9. Brer Lion listened to Brer Rabbit's advice; however, he later realized he'd been tricked.
10. Writer Amy Ling lives in the United States, yet she was born in Beijing, China.

EXERCISE C *(If you permit students to omit the final series comma, then the commas that are underscored below may be considered optional.)*

One hundred years ago there were a hundred thousand elephants living in Asia; however, now there are only about one third of that number. What an alarming loss! The Asian elephant is now an endangered species for the following reasons: cutting of forests, other damage to habitat, and increased human population. Of the Asian elephants that remain, about ten thousand live in the small country of Myanmar. Can you find it on a map? It is between Thailand and Bangladesh. Many of the huge, patient elephants, also called timber elephants, work with humans; together they bring in large, valuable trees to sell for lumber. Elephants and people have a partnership, and they spend their lives together. This partnership is remarkable for the mutual affection and trust it demonstrates between animals and humans.

EXERCISE D *(If you permit students to omit the final series comma, then the commas that are underscored below may be considered optional.)*

August 18, 2000

Dear Nolan,

Jovita told me that you are interested in joining the Environmental Club. Welcome aboard! Beginning Sept. 10, 2000, we will meet each Thursday after school at the recycling center at 1651 Yeager Ave. At each meeting progress reports are given, activities are discussed, and plans are made. We also have some social time, of course, and everyone enjoys the meetings. The club's goal is to make our town litter-free, and so far we have made a lot of progress. Jovita, the other members of the club, and I look forward to having you as a part of our group.

Sincerely,

Gwynneth

EXERCISE E *(If you permit students to omit the final series comma, then the commas that are underscored below may be considered optional.)*

September 5, 2000

Dear Customer Service Representative:

Recently I called about my food processor, which has the following defects: The container lid flies off when the power is turned on, the speed is always fast regardless of the button pushed, and smoke pours out of the motor. Your manual "Food Processors: How to Enjoy Them" has not been much help at all. Although most manuals have a section that describes what to do about possible problems, this manual does not.

When I called, you said the manager would contact me; furthermore, you said the manager would have someone from the Small Appliance Repair Department call me. Neither has happened, and three months seems long enough to wait.

The food processor was purchased April 3; the problems began July 5, a few days after the ninety-day warranty expired. While I realize that these things happen, your company's lack of response has had the following effect: It has caused me to lose confidence in your company, your company's advertising, your company's reliability, and your company's products.

Please contact me before I vow never to buy your company's products again.

Sincerely,

Phyllis Freeman

LANGUAGE HANDBOOK 14 PUNCTUATION

WORKSHEET 1
Using Italics

EXERCISE

1. g, q
2. *Porgy and Bess*
3. *The Loon Feather*
4. *Sunset Limited*
5. *access*
6. *Woman Ironing*
7. *Pocahontas, Mulan*
8. *Discovery*
9. *cheap, inexpensive*
10. *USA Today*
11. *Frasier*
12. *Queen Mary*
13. *The Incredible Journey*
14. *The Call of the Wild*
15. *Field of Dreams*
16. *Aida*
17. *supersede, sede*
18. *Chant*
19. *The Nutcracker*
20. *The Fellowship of the Ring*
21. *The Miracle Worker*
22. *Flyer*
23. *ough, cough, bough, enough, through*
24. *Time Out of Mind*
25. 6, 9

WORKSHEET 2
Punctuating Quotations

EXERCISE A

1. "What was it?" asked Gary.
2. "It was *Babe,* the movie about an orphaned pig," replied Leah.
3. "Oh, I love that film!" exclaimed Tammy.
4. "Did you know there was a sequel?" asked Gary.
5. Tammy said, "I like the original movie best."
6. "I like adventure films better than comedies," stated Gary.
7. I
8. "I think *Raiders of the Lost Ark* with Harrison Ford is my favorite," he replied.
9. Leah inquired, "Did you see *Gone with the Wind* on television?"
10. I

EXERCISE B

1. "Are you going to try out for the school play?" asked Dawn.
2. "I would love to be in it, but I'm afraid I would freeze on the stage," said Imala.
3. "That is all the more reason for auditioning," replied Dawn.
4. Ernesto said, "You have to face your fears in order to conquer them."
5. "You would be perfect for the role of Sabina in *The Skin of Our Teeth*," responded Dawn.
6. Imala said, "That's the role I wanted."
7. "Ernesto, are you going to audition for the role of Mr. Anthropus?" inquired Dawn.
8. "I sure am!" exclaimed Ernesto.
9. "Wow, that's great because I'm trying out for the part of Mrs. Anthropus!" exclaimed Dawn.
10. "Then we may all be in the play together," said Imala.

WORKSHEET 3
Punctuating Quotations and Dialogue

EXERCISE A

1. "About how long a trip will it be?" asked Charlotte.
2. "It's about twelve miles," replied Paul. "We will have to prepare for an all-day trip."
3. "We'll need two adults to come with us," commented Sharon, "since they will have to rent the canoes and provide supervision."
4. Ms. Roth, the supervisor of the Backwoods Canoe Club, replied, "I, of course, will be glad to come. Mr. Spenser, the mathematics teacher, canoed down that part of the river last year."
5. "Should we ask Mr. Spenser to come with us?" asked Annette.
6. "That sounds like a good idea," said Ms. Roth. "I'll personally ask him to come."
7. "We should make a map of the area," said Dennis. "We could indicate where to expect white water."
8. Charlotte added, "We could also show points along the land bordering the river that would help us know where we are."
9. "We could arrange for a speaker to talk to the club about handling a canoe in white water," suggested Ms. Roth.
10. "My parents are excellent canoeists," said Dennis. "They would be glad to come to talk to us."

Answer Key **45**

LANGUAGE HANDBOOK 14 PUNCTUATION

EXERCISE B

"I propose that we take a canoe trip down the Delaware!" (*or* Delaware,") said Paul with enthusiasm. "We could rent the canoes in Callicoon and paddle down to Bingham Falls."

¶ "I think that's a good idea," said Charlotte, "but how do we get the canoes back to Callicoon?"

¶ "That's easy," said Paul. "There is a series of posts along the river where we can leave the canoes. We rent them at one post and check them in at a post farther down the river."

¶ "Should we schedule the trip for next week?" asked Bruce.

WORKSHEET 4
Using Italics and Quotation Marks

EXERCISE

1. "Mother said to me, 'Act now,'" said Vincente.
2. The first chapter of the Dickens novel <u>David Copperfield</u> is titled "I Am Born."
3. Last night Frank saw an old episode of <u>Star Trek</u> called "The Trouble with Tribbles."
4. "Vegetarians should like the poem 'Point of View,' shouldn't they?" asked Mr. Gable.
5. The magazine article titled "Aliens Have Landed!" caught my attention.
6. Annie said, "My favorite poem begins 'Once upon a midnight dreary.'"
7. O. Henry's "The Ransom of Red Chief" is a hilarious short story.
8. Mrs. Nelson asked us to read the poem "They Have Yarns" by Carl Sandburg.
9. Isn't "Camp Harmony" an excerpt from the book <u>Nisei Daughter</u>?
10. She can't remember who originally wrote and performed the song "Something."
11. I believe it's on the Beatles album <u>Abbey Road</u>.
12. My uncle John is a correspondent for the magazine <u>U.S. News & World Report</u>.
13. There is an article in today's <u>New York Times</u> titled "Metropolitan Museum Names Two New Leaders."
14. "Have you ever heard about the famous train <u>The City of New Orleans</u>?" asked Kathryn.
15. The famous painting <u>Mona Lisa</u> is on display at the Louvre in Paris, France.
16. This year the Paramount Theater is going to host a production of <u>The Phantom of the Opera</u>.
17. My favorite song from <u>The Sound of Music</u> is "My Favorite Things."
18. "The poem 'I've Known Rivers,'" said Mr. Grainger, "comes from the book <u>The Big Sea</u> by Langston Hughes."
19. "What is the Shakespeare play," said Maria, "that includes the speech that begins 'Tomorrow and tomorrow and tomorrow'?"
20. "I think it's <u>Macbeth</u>," replied Jeff.

WORKSHEET 5
Test

EXERCISE A

1. "How many pounds are you pressing during workouts?" Mom asked.
2. "William," Mrs. Winters asked, "when will you learn?"
3. "The whole school will participate in Black History Month," the principal said.
4. "Sharon wants to take ballet," Mrs. Wright said, "but she has twisted her ankle."
5. Ron asked, "Does anyone know the poem that begins 'A new day is dawning'?"
6. "An old sock," Andrew exclaimed, "is stuck in the drainpipe!"
7. "This German potato salad is delicious," Marlene said. "May I have the recipe?"
8. "The city council voted to review the city's position," Clay announced.
9. "What did Jane mean," asked Rachel, "when she said that Rose will know?"
10. Marcella replied, "The song is titled 'On Higher Ground.'"

EXERCISE B

1. "Indeed," Miss Bursa replied, "the Japanese yen is rising."
2. "People are generally quite hopeful," the speaker said.
3. C
4. Paul said that the train doesn't stop here anymore.
5. "Laws are for your protection," the police officer said, "not your inconvenience."
6. Cody Ray said that the story of the laughing fence post is a myth.
7. C

46 *Language Handbook Worksheets*

LANGUAGE HANDBOOK 14 PUNCTUATION

8. **"**The game's on, rain or shine!**"** Trevor yelled.
9. Mr. Lindt suggested that we try out for the debate team.
10. **"**I know the community will help the family,**"** Reverend Marshall said.

EXERCISE C

"You said your parents own a kosher deli, Rachel. What does that mean?**"** Diane asked.

"It means that it's a Jewish deli,**"** Rachel replied.

"Yes, I understand that. But what is *kosher*?**"** Diane asked.

"Oh, it means that some food is prepared in certain ways,**"** Rachel said.

"How?**"** Diane asked. **"**According to what standards?**"**

"Jewish religious rules say how some food is to be prepared,**"** Rachel explained. **"**There are special recipes.**"**

"Sounds interesting!**"** Diane said. **"**What are some of the foods that I could buy at the deli?**"**

"Well, I will tell you my favorite thing to get,**"** Rachel said. **"**I love potato knishes!**"**

"I've never had them, or even heard of them,**"** Diane said. **"**What are they?**"**

"They're pastries filled with potatoes. I'll treat you to one after school today,**"** Rachel said.

EXERCISE D

1. Diego Rivera's expressive painting <u>The Grinder</u> depicts a woman making tortillas.
2. Barbara won't leave home without her <u>Rand McNally Road Atlas</u>.
3. Ogden Nash, in his poem **"**The Panther,**"** created the word <u>anther</u>.
4. The song **"**Tomorrow**"** is from the Broadway musical <u>Annie</u>.
5. I clipped the article **"**Reuse or Recycle**"** from today's <u>Kansas City Star</u> for our talk.
6. In Jules Verne's novel <u>Twenty Thousand Leagues Under the Sea</u>, the submarine is named the <u>Nautilus</u>.
7. When taking notes, some people distinguish between the capital letter <u>O</u> and the numeral <u>0</u> by drawing a <u>/</u> through the numeral.
8. Toni Cade Bambara's book <u>Gorilla, My Love</u> has many wonderful short stories in it.
9. Some people pronounce short <u>e</u>'s and <u>i</u>'s the same in words like <u>pin</u> and <u>pen</u>.
10. Have you seen the dance production called <u>Stomp</u>?

Answer Key **47**

LANGUAGE HANDBOOK 15 PUNCTUATION

WORKSHEET 1
Using Apostrophes to Show Possession

EXERCISE A
1. dog's tail; dogs' tails
2. son's smile; sons' smiles
3. cat's eye; cats' eyes
4. sister's task; sisters' tasks
5. detective's question; detectives' questions
6. house's chimney; houses' chimneys
7. doctor's car; doctors' cars
8. neighbor's yard; neighbors' yards
9. baby's bottle; babies' bottles
10. mouse's squeak; mice's squeaks

EXERCISE B
1. Rachel's and Paul's papers are on Miss Conway's desk, but ours aren't.
2. One of the boys had lost his father's jacket.
3. What shall we do with the geese's feathers?
4. In the Middle Ages a goose's feathers were used to make arrows.
5. A pelican's beak is more than a foot long, and a pouch hangs from the lower part of the beak.
6. Our grandparents' old schoolbooks look dull compared with today's.
7. Please tell me the company's address.
8. What have they predicted for tomorrow's weather?
9. He is so quick that he does about eight hours' work in three hours.
10. Our town's oldest house is out on the river road.

WORKSHEET 2
Using Apostrophes for Contractions, Plurals, and Possessives

EXERCISE A
1. you are
2. she would (*or* she had)
3. did not
4. was not
5. do not
6. is not
7. we are
8. has not
9. he will
10. you will

EXERCISE B
1. aren't
2. it's
3. she'll
4. there's
5. they're
6. he'd
7. let's
8. where's
9. '70
10. we'd

EXERCISE C
1. its
2. they're
3. their
4. Whose
5. who's
6. It's
7. You're
8. your
9. It's
10. their

EXERCISE D
1. There are two *c*'s and two *r*'s in the word *occurring*.
2. Wherever we have lived, there have always been two *6*'s in our address.
3. Some authors prefer to use *&*'s instead of *and*'s in their titles.
4. Try not to use too many *well*'s in your speech.
5. Two *o*'s give Geronimo's name an interesting sound.
6. Ellen's Social Security number contains four *7*'s.
7. How many *@*'s are in an e-mail address?
8. "Your *e*'s look too much like your *i*'s, Randall," said Ms. Yang.
9. Four *the*'s in your title are too many, in my opinion.
10. Counting by *9*'s is difficult even for some adults.

EXERCISE E
1. My oldest brother's pet mice are as big as yours.
2. There are two pairs of men's overalls hanging behind the barn door.
3. Marie didn't give the problem a moment's thought.
4. The mayor's friends formed a citizens' committee to reelect her.
5. Have you seen today's newspapers anywhere?
6. Ralph's bicycle is in better condition than theirs are.
7. Someone left the dog's leash on the front porch.
8. The children's toys were scattered behind the sofa.

48 Language Handbook Worksheets

LANGUAGE HANDBOOK 15 PUNCTUATION

9. Our city's tallest buildings have all been built recently.
10. The twins' mother has won an award for her story.

WORKSHEET 3
Using Hyphens
EXERCISE A
1. chop-sticks
2. dar-ling
3. Ger-ma-ny
4. po-si-tion
5. sphinx
6. brother-in-law
7. kite
8. tech-ni-cal
9. Per-sian
10. ce-ment

EXERCISE B
1. for thirty-three years
2. C
3. every fifty-five minutes
4. only one-half liter
5. one-fourth full
6. C
7. C
8. C
9. two-thirds cup
10. with forty-one dollars

WORKSHEET 4
Using Parentheses and Dashes
EXERCISE (Sentences 1, 4, 9, 11, 17, 20, 24, and 25 are correct with either dashes or parentheses.)
1. Tell me——I doubt that you can——what city is the capital of Wyoming.
2. Gouda (pronounced gouʹdə) is a kind of cheese.
3. The correct answer appears to be——no, figure it out for yourself.
4. Sludge——the word itself sounds horrid——filled our basement during the flood.
5. Movie producer Samuel Goldwyn (1882-1974) was born in Poland.
6. Brenda can't——that is, won't——help me.
7. The box contains a pound (16 ounces) of detergent.
8. Cajun music——how I love it!——is loud and lively.
9. Gila monsters——they give me the shivers——aren't really monsters.
10. They are classified as lizards (the biological family Helodermatidae).
11. My desk calendar (it was a gift) contains animal cartoons.
12. "Next we will read——please stop talking——from the book," Mr. Naylor said.
13. My grandfather's first truck (a Chevrolet) is worth a lot now.
14. The right solution to your problem——I repeat——will come to you.
15. The winning number is——but first, a commercial break.
16. The marching band——can you believe it?——actually won first place.
17. Derek——I think you've met him——enjoys racing automobiles.
18. My dream——I don't care if you do laugh——is to be a professional clown.
19. San Marino (population 24,000) is a small independent country.
20. The restored house——it has always been a favorite of mine——is now a museum.
21. This picture is of a three-toed sloth (species *Bradypus*).
22. Sloths——believe it or not——feed while hanging down from branches.
23. Khalil Gibran (1883-1931) was a writer and artist from Lebanon.
24. Have patience (easier said than done) and you'll succeed.
25. One of our cats——the gray one——often hid under the couch.

WORKSHEET 5
Test
EXERCISE A
1. CON—she's
2. PL—5's
3. POS—geese's
4. CON—shouldn't
5. CON—they're
6. POS—*fox's* den
7. CON—who's
8. CON—summer of '99

Answer Key **49**

LANGUAGE HANDBOOK 15 PUNCTUATION

9. CON—wasn't
10. PL—recite your *abc*'s
11. POS—two *monkeys'* food
12. POS—*Rover's* doghouse
13. CON—*it's* snowing
14. POS—one *girl's* uniform
15. PL—*6's* and *7's*
16. CON—you're
17. POS—*family's* trip
18. POS—many *voters'* rights
19. CON—you'll
20. CON—*that's* right
21. PL—dot those *i's* and *j's*
22. POS—*fish's* habitat
23. POS—*nobody's* fault
24. CON—*here's* the food
25. POS—*children's* playground

EXERCISE B

1. boy's
2. men's
3. persons'
4. books'
5. oxen's
6. moose's
7. poet's
8. children's
9. animals'
10. year's
11. everybody's
12. mother's
13. students'
14. churches'
15. Ross's
16. artists'
17. countries'
18. videos'
19. someone's
20. sheep's

EXERCISE C

1. We'd
2. It'll
3. isn't
4. It's
5. You'd
6. doesn't
7. Where's
8. won't
9. They'd
10. Haven't

EXERCISE D *(Students do not have to hyphenate words at every syllable, just in one correct place.)*

1. per-son-al
2. forge
3. mu-si-cal
4. C
5. brother-in-law
6. car-rot
7. mon-key
8. ex-treme-ly
9. pas-sen-ger
10. moth-er

EXERCISE E *(Sentences 3 and 7 are correct with either dashes or parentheses.)*

1. Pesto (pronounced pes´to) is a sauce made with basil, garlic, pine nuts, and olive oil.
2. "We are leaving on the 12:45——no, 1:45 P.M.——flight to Chicago," John said.
3. I like the long, hooded cloaks (called *burnooses*) worn by some Arabs.
4. The clock——its chiming drives me crazy——was a gift.
5. The Dales——correct me if I am wrong——are on vacation.
6. Easter Island (also known as Rapa Nui) is inhabited by about two thousand people.
7. The star of the concert——you would have loved him——was the jazz saxophonist.
8. Frances Perkins was U.S. Secretary of Labor (1933-1945) under Franklin Roosevelt.
9. The next assignment will be——where is my book?
10. The winter solstice (the shortest day of the year) ended with a beautiful sunset.

50 Language Handbook Worksheets

LANGUAGE HANDBOOK 16 SPELLING

WORKSHEET 1
Using Word Parts

EXERCISE *(Definitions will vary somewhat.)*
1. mis | lead—to direct the course of wrongly
2. im | port—to carry in
3. dif | fuse—to melt or spread out in different directions
4. re | try—attempt again
5. at | tract | ion—the act or state of drawing toward
6. dis | like—not to have a preference or fondness for
7. post | script—something written after
8. fear | ful—full of a feeling of anxiety caused by a perception of danger
9. port | er—one who carries
10. spectat | or—one who sees or watches
11. dis | trust—not to have faith in or be confident of
12. mis | place—to put in a particular place wrongly
13. dict | ion—manner of speaking or pointing out in words
14. ex | port—to carry out of
15. tempera | ment—the result of the mixture of ingredients in a person's nature or personality
16. re | state—to say again
17. health | ful—full of a state of being sound, whole
18. dis | quali | fy—to make not fit for or deprive of a specific right to
19. re | place—to put in a particular location again
20. port | able—able to be carried
21. trans | scribe—to write in full or across to the other side of
22. re | spect—to look back on
23. cheer | ful—full of face or mood; full of good feeling
24. translat | or—one who carries across from one language to another
25. forma | tion—the act of giving shape

WORKSHEET 2
Spelling Words with *ie, ei, cede, ceed,* and *sede*

EXERCISE A
1. receipt
2. tie
3. proceed
4. science
5. leisure
6. deficient
7. secede
8. view
9. height
10. relieve
11. achievement
12. either
13. perceive
14. exceed
15. inconceivable
16. supersede
17. weird
18. intercede
19. niece
20. neigh

EXERCISE B *(The first item in a pair is correct. The second is incorrect.)*
1. premiere—premeire
2. patiently—pateintly
3. precedes—preceeds
4. C
5. Neither—Niether
6. succeed—succede
7. freight—frieght
8. foreign-language—foriegn-language
9. C
10. weight—wieght

WORKSHEET 3
Adding Prefixes and Suffixes

EXERCISE A
1. outrageous
2. sleepily
3. strayed
4. misstate
5. daily
6. normally
7. boxing
8. drying
9. illogical
10. tuneless
11. rotten
12. argument
13. knitting
14. overrule
15. diving
16. busily
17. frankness
18. buying
19. tardiness
20. barely

Answer Key 51

LANGUAGE HANDBOOK 16 SPELLING

EXERCISE B *(The first item in a pair is correct. The second is incorrect.)*
1. override—overide
2. noticeable—noticable
3. C
4. leading—leadding
5. happened—happenned
6. adorable—adoreable
7. giving—giveing
8. hurried—hurryed
9. Evenness—Eveness
10. C

WORKSHEET 4
Forming the Plurals of Nouns

EXERCISE A
1. wives
2. oxen
3. raceways
4. Japanese
5. candles
6. counties
7. *z*'s
8. wishes
9. children
10. Carys
11. rodeos
12. two-year-olds
13. boxes
14. Zorros
15. *4*'s
16. sons-in-law
17. Johnsons
18. potatoes
19. navies
20. *%*'s

EXERCISE B *(The first item in a pair is correct. The second is incorrect.)*
1. horseshoes—horsesshoe
2. C
3. sisters-in-law—sister-in-laws
4. leaves—leafs
5. feet—foots
6. Chinese—Chineses
7. Mercados, Inc.—Mercadoes, Inc.
8. monkeys—monkeies
9. C
10. stereos—stereoes

WORKSHEET 5
More Practice Forming the Plurals of Nouns and Spelling Numbers

EXERCISE A
1. mice
2. cities
3. sopranos
4. wrenches
5. thirteen-year-olds
6. Wileys
7. briefs
8. *hello*'s
9. tomatoes
10. lilies
11. butterflies
12. topazes
13. Vietnamese
14. Neros
15. spacecraft
16. men
17. lives
18. igloos
19. galleys
20. sit-ups

EXERCISE B *(The first item in a pair is correct. The second is incorrect.)*
1. trophies—trophys
2. rains—raines
3. ditches—ditchs
4. waltzes—waltzs
5. C
6. two—2
7. *s*'s—*s*'
8. third—3rd
9. C
10. One hundred—100

WORKSHEET 6
Test

EXERCISE A *(The first item in a pair is correct. The second is incorrect.)*
1. intercede—interceed
2. axes—axs
3. can openers—cans opener
4. C
5. allies—allys
6. interchangeable—interchangable
7. oxen—ox
8. two—2
9. C
10. C (*or* volcanos)

52 *Language Handbook Worksheets*

Language Handbook 16: Spelling

EXERCISE B *(The first item in a pair is correct. The second is incorrect.)*
1. twenty-two—22
2. concede—conceed
3. creativity—creativeity
4. studios—studioes
5. variety—vareity
6. students—studentes
7. overrun—overun
8. easily—easyly
9. ninth—9th
10. Saturdays—Saturdayes

EXERCISE C *(The first item in a pair is correct. The second is incorrect.)*
1. patios—patioes
2. supplies—supplys
3. Fifteen—15
4. ancient—anceint
5. C
6. aircraft—aircrafts
7. C
8. brothers-in-law—brother-in-laws
9. roofs—rooves
10. superseded—superceded

EXERCISE D *(The first item in a pair is correct. The second is incorrect.)*
1. succeeded—succeded
2. C
3. stories—storys
4. Happily—Happyly
5. starred—stared; comedies—comedys
6. received—recieved
7. series—serieses
8. parenting—parentting
9. men—mans
10. truly—truely

Answer Key **53**

LANGUAGE HANDBOOK 17 GLOSSARY OF USAGE

WORKSHEET 1
Common Usage Problems
EXERCISE
1. fewer
2. well
3. ought
4. Jones
5. A lot
6. than
7. A
8. among
9. chose
10. as if
11. badly
12. very
13. that
14. inside
15. himself
16. taught
17. isn't
18. broke
19. somewhat
20. except
21. effect
22. altogether
23. ought not
24. why
25. somewhat

WORKSHEET 2
Common Usage Problems
EXERCISE
1. have
2. rather
3. bad
4. effects
5. less
6. those
7. why
8. choose
9. all together
10. well
11. Advertisers
12. As
13. that
14. already
15. burst
16. try to
17. a pupil who
18. is
19. themselves
20. off
21. than
22. somewhat
23. teach
24. very
25. have

WORKSHEET 3
Test
EXERCISE A
1. outside
2. already
3. friends
4. somewhat
5. as
6. well
7. than
8. between
9. effect
10. less

EXERCISE B *(The first item in a pair is correct. The second is incorrect.)*
1. badly—bad
2. must have heard—must of heard
3. why—how come
4. very (*or* extremely)—real
5. as if—like
6. C
7. accepted—excepted
8. altogether—all together
9. was...born?—was...born at?
10. that—because

EXERCISE C
1. bad
2. that
3. well
4. broke
5. An
6. should have
7. all ready
8. am not
9. themselves
10. excepted

EXERCISE D *(The first item in a pair is correct. The second is incorrect.)*
1. broke—busted
2. rather (*or* somewhat)—sort of
3. is an exchange—is when there is an exchange
4. C
5. affects—effects
6. among—between
7. C
8. rather (*or* somewhat)—kind of
9. chose—choose
10. oughtn't (*or* ought not)—hadn't ought to

54 Language Handbook Worksheets